# TRADING
# WITH OSCILLATORS

## Wiley Trader's Exchange Series

# TRADING WITH OSCILLATORS

## PINPOINTING MARKET EXTREMES— THEORY AND PRACTICE

### MARK ETZKORN

**JOHN WILEY & SONS, INC.**

NEW YORK • CHICHESTER • WEINHEIM • BRISBANE • SINGAPORE • TORONTO

# FOR MINA

Copyright © 1997 by Mark Etzkorn. All rights reserved.
Published by John Wiley & Sons, Inc.
Published simultaneously in Canada.

This publication is designed to provide accurate and authoritative information in regard to the subject matter covered. It is sold with the understanding that the publisher is not engaged in rendering legal, accounting, or other professional services. If legal advice or other expert assistance is required, the services of a competent professional person should be sought.

*Library of Congress Cataloging-in-Publication Data:*
Etzkorn, Mark.
    Trading with oscillators : pinpointing market extremes—theory and practice / Mark Etzkorn.
       p.  cm.
    Includes index.
    ISBN 0-471-15538-1 (pbk. : alk. paper)
    1. Investment analysis.   I. Title.
HG4529.E89   1997
332.6—dc21                 97-22410

Printed in the United States of America.
10 9 8 7 6 5 4 3

# CONTENTS

**6**

## Innovations and Modifications    75

**7**

## Other Issues: Divergence, Longer Time Frames, and Price Inputs    105

**8**

## Conclusion: Oscillators in Context    125

**9**

## Other Oscillators    129

# ACKNOWLEDGMENTS

Plenty of thanks must be passed around: Cynthia Kase, Martin Pring, William Blau, Tushar Chande, and Tom DeMark all provided generous feedback regarding their work. George Pruitt of FuturesTruth (as always) offered his time and insight to testing matters. Thanks also to Omega Research, Equis International, FutureSource, and Gary Wagner at International Pacific Trading Company for technical and graphic support, and the staff of *Futures* magazine for their support and access to their resources. Thanks to Mahendra Jain for his input.

Special thanks to Tom DeMark and Pamela van Giessen (and John Wiley & Sons) for making this project possible.

# INTRODUCTION

Technical analysis is a difficult subject for a novice to approach. Literature on the subject is abundant, but frequently confusing. Simple concepts sometimes get buried in an avalanche of dense jargon, complex equations, and numerous interpretive rules (as well as exceptions to those rules). At the other end of the spectrum lie generalizations that only superficially address the intricacies of a given trading situation. Also, a popular trading idea or indicator can (by chance or promotion) obtain a life and mystique completely unrelated to its merit in the markets. Finally, the sometimes considerable gap between theory and practice (that is, between analysis and trading) is frequently overlooked.

Few technical indicators are as popular as the group of related tools known as momentum oscillators—reflected by the abundance of book and magazine pages devoted to them as well as their prevalence in trading software and analysis packages. Many of these tools, as well as general interpretations of the momentum concept, have become part of commonly accepted technical wisdom. Not surprisingly, the great popularity of these indicators is probably equaled only by the magnitude of the misunderstandings surrounding them.

Ironically, this may be due in part to the power of the computer technology that has enabled people to view, test, and design technical indicators with ease and flexibility that was unimaginable just a few years ago. While this has undoubtedly heightened the popularity of technical analysis, it also has distanced many traders from the basic construction, underlying logic, and subtleties of the tools they use. Many of today's most popular indicators were designed years ago by traders and analysts who had to painstakingly calculate and plot their studies on a daily basis. That kind of hands-on experience creates a much deeper appreciation and understanding of an indicator than simply clicking a button. For the modern user, complacency often results. Users who have had to put little effort into the analytical process are disinclined to scratch very far beneath the surface of ideas and methods.

This book is designed for readers comfortable with at least the fundamentals of technical analysis who are perhaps a little confused about momentum and the dizzying array of oscillators available in charting and analysis programs. It is intended to help the reader gain a solid understanding of the basic concepts underpinning these indicators, an appreciation of their important differences (and similarities), and an awareness of the issues that impact their application in the markets. Additionally, the reader will be introduced to some of the more recent innovations in this area of technical analysis. Ultimately, this information provides a departure point for further research and experimentation. The reader will be educated enough to make up his or her own mind about the value of these tools, pursue more advanced study, and be better able to use these tools successfully. Issues will be discussed in plain language as much as possible, with complex math and formulas kept to a minimum (except in cases where it is unavoidable). The information is structured in pyramid fashion: first laying a foundation of simple concepts, then gradually adding successive levels of more complex and sophisticated material.

Many books that delve into one or more specific areas of momentum and oscillators in greater technical detail are readily available through bookstores and financial publishers. For those desiring further study, several are listed in the bibliography. Most of the indicators outlined in this book can be calculated with a spreadsheet program. The reader (especially the less-experienced reader) may find it helpful to take the time to program the various tools in this book so they are not merely words on a page or lines on a chart. This dissection process acquaints the trader with all the working parts of an indicator, and how they come together to reflect price action.

This book presents information more from a trading perspective than an analytical one. Although trading and analysis may seem inseparable, this is not necessarily the case, as evidenced by a common division of labor on the institutional level: A trading firm may employ full-time analysts (who have never traded) to generate market forecasts, full-time traders who design and implement strategy based on this information, and full-time brokers who execute the trades without having any opinion about them. Many people (rightly) associate analysis with an ongoing process of forecasting future price action. Successful trading, however, may or may not incorporate such forecasts. For example, even if accurate, a particular forecast may be too vague to translate into an effective trading plan that requires strict risk control or time limits.

The demands of trading and analysis are quite different. Not all good analysts are good traders. Good traders, on the other hand, by definition must be good analysts. Discounting blind luck, whatever conclusions they have come to about the markets have resulted in sustained, profitable trading. This result is not one of the barometers of market success, it's the *only* barometer.

As a result, many observations in the following pages address some of the practical challenges of objectively and systematically *trading* with certain tools as opposed to subjectively and discretionarily *forecasting* with them. The goal is not to slight either subjectivity or forecasting. There are nontrading analysts and forecasters who nonetheless have sustained track records supporting the value of their forecasts and trade recommendations. Several of the most successful traders I have met (or heard about) are discretionary traders, although in at least some cases their basic methodologies could probably be reduced to a few core rules that form the foundation of a system. However, I believe a systematic approach offers the best chance of success for the greatest number of traders—systematic in this case not excluding discretion, but rather referring to replicable and unambiguous trading rules that form the basis of a trading approach and that have at least a minimal proven reliability (i.e., profitability) in historical testing or real-time trading.

Furthermore, a good way to develop a sense of an indicator's strengths and weaknesses is to see how its basic trade signals perform when applied in an objective, systematic fashion (if that is possible). While such testing may not reveal the best use of a tool, it at least provides a benchmark—a perspective from which to understand its function, improve its performance, and incorporate it most effectively into a trading plan. In other words, knowing why and when an approach is unlikely to work is a useful step toward finding a solution to a trading problem.

There are a few areas in life for which books are the ultimate source of knowledge. For the historian, written materials may be the primary source of information through which a subject is mastered and ideas developed. Not so for the trader. When approaching the markets, books are only a first step and should always be considered second-hand information—however useful. Unlike the historian, every trader has the opportunity to hear (and judge) firsthand the words of the original "source"—the markets.

Books are like indicators themselves. They may have value in certain contexts or circumstances, but there isn't one that is a panacea for all (or even most) trading challenges. Books should be the departure point for any trader's study of price action and market behavior—not the ultimate destination. Readers should endeavor to discover for themselves the realities of technical analysis and the value of any trading idea. The information in these pages will help people learn about momentum-based indicators, sift through some of the confusing and often contradictory information regarding them, and as a result enjoy more realistic market analysis and trading.

*A note on testing and software:* Original indicator tests summarized in this book were performed in Omega Research's TradeStation and Dialectical System's Market Sage. Unless otherwise noted, daily continuous futures data from April 2, 1984, through March 31, 1994, was used. Equis International's MetaStock program and FuturesTruth's Excalibur program were used for additional indicator construction and testing.

Futures markets were used in testing for simplicity's sake. Individual stock and mutual fund examples are included in the book to demonstrate that the indicators are applicable to all markets.

# 1

# MOMENTUM: DEFINITIONS AND BASIC CONCEPTS

Before discussing a technical indicator or a trading approach, it's helpful to understand the basic concepts upon which it's based. Those indicators commonly lumped together under the banner of momentum oscillators have at their core a fundamental aspect of price behavior, *momentum*, which refers to the rate at which prices change rather than absolute price differences. It is often compared to speed ($s$) or velocity: $s = d/t$, where $d$ is the distance covered and $t$ is time. In market terms, momentum ($m$) can be defined by substituting the change in price of a particular asset for the change in distance in the speed formula: $m = \Delta p/t$, where $\Delta p$ is the change in price and $t$ is time. Momentum's significance lies in the information it conveys about price direction and strength; it can measure both the direction and strength of a particular price move, two key pieces of trading information.

Momentum is closely tied to the concepts of trend and directional price movement. The distinguishing characteristic of a trend is sustained price gains or losses over a particular time period. If the price of a particular instrument rises from

10 to 100, the absolute price difference is 90; this change, however, represents a completely different type of market environment if it occurs over 10 days than if it occurs over 10 weeks. The greater the directional price change over a given time period, the greater the speed, or momentum, of the market. From a longer-term perspective, strong momentum implies a healthy price trend; weak momentum suggests a price move that may be approaching its end—in the form of a temporary pause, a short-term correction, or a reversal. However, extreme momentum readings often accompany shorter-term exhaustion points, identifying places where a market may be overextended (having risen or fallen too far too fast) and is due for a correction. It's important to note that although these price/ momentum relationships are common and easily observable, they are not universal; important exceptions exist. The degree to which different momentum indicators reflect these market dynamics and the ability of traders to profit from them is at the heart of momentum analysis.

There are any number of ways to calculate momentum (as evidenced by the variety of oscillator studies available in charting and analysis software programs). The most basic calculation—and the one that usually bears the name momentum—is the difference between the current price and the price $n$ days in the past (the closing price of a standard bar chart is most commonly used). A 10-day momentum calculation would be the difference between the close today and the close 10 days ago (any time period—month, week, hour—can be substituted). The difference between the two prices—a measurement of how much price changed over this period—will be positive or negative depending on whether the current close is higher or lower than the close 10 days ago.

Figure 1.1 shows a hypothetical price series with a 1-day momentum calculation (price today − price yesterday). Successively larger positive momentum readings reflect prices rising at an increasing rate, while successively larger negative momentum values accompany prices falling at an increasing rate. A market that rises 3 points one day, 5 the next day, 8 the next, and 12 the next, for example, is obviously moving with greater

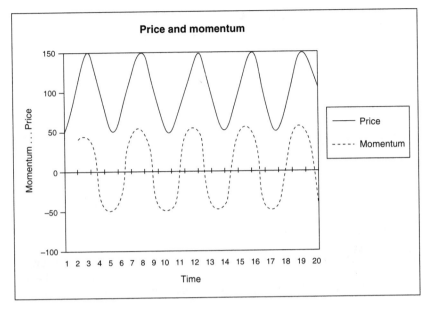

**FIGURE 1.1** Hypothetical Price Series with a One-Day Momentum Calculation

force—greater momentum—than a market rising 1 point per day. Figure 1.2 shows how a 20-period momentum study highlights waning trend strength in a weekly chart of the S&P 500 stock index. The momentum values remain positive for most of the example, meaning prices have stayed above their levels of 20 days earlier. As time passes, however, the degree to which they are higher decreases, indicated by the down-sloping momentum peak trendline. Momentum is weakening.

## MOMENTUM CHARACTERISTICS

A common momentum analogy is the behavior of a ball or some other object launched into the air. Consider an arrow shot skyward: Its momentum is greatest just as it leaves the bowstring and gradually decreases until reaching zero at the height of its trajectory—immediately before the arrow returns to earth.

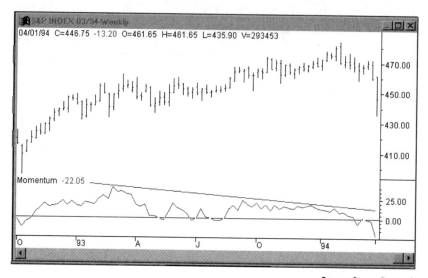

**FIGURE 1.2**    Twenty-Period Momentum Study

A price trend often (but not always) exhibits the same momentum characteristics. At the beginning of a trend, as price reverses the previous trend or breaks out from an extended trading range, a market will frequently exhibit its strongest momentum. As the trend progresses, it may do so at a slower rate—prices continue to rise or fall, but in smaller increments from day to day (or week to week, etc.). Like the arrow that gradually loses speed until its velocity reaches zero at the peak of its flight, a price trend may exhibit flattened or even declining momentum as it approaches its conclusion—sometimes *reversing before price itself reverses*. Such momentum characteristics, which may not be immediately evident through basic trend analysis or price chart inspection, can provide advance warning of a trend change or pause.

Unlike an arrow shot into the sky, however, price trends do not follow smooth lines or curves; in all but the most perfect situations, they advance and retrace, or pause, before resuming the previous trend or beginning a new one in the opposite direction. As mentioned, a basic function of momentum studies is to identify points (shorter-term points, especially) where a market has become overextended or exhausted (*overbought* or *oversold*). This type of analysis is based on the concept that a market rising or falling too far too fast—that is, a market exhibiting extremely strong momentum—cannot sustain its pace indefinitely and will at least temporarily pause or reverse, providing the trader with advantageous points at which to enter or exit positions. The most basic interpretation is to sell a market that is overbought and buy a market that is oversold. This is, in essence, contrarian, or countertrend trading. It implies anticipating future price direction and establishing a position against the current trend.

Any number of technical studies called *momentum oscillators* quantify this aspect of price behavior. They are referred to as oscillators because they generally fluctuate (in idealized form like a sine wave) above and below a horizontal line that represents equivalent price levels and zero momentum (i.e., a momentum equilibrium point, where momentum is neither increasing nor decreasing). In contrast to trend-following tools like moving averages, which identify the direction of the market and allow traders to participate in the trend, momentum oscillators are generally used as countertrend tools to find market extremes or exhaustion points—or to identify the end of trending moves as momentum dissipates. (As we will see, however, momentum oscillators can also function as trend indicators.) Accordingly, they are commonly recommended for use in markets swinging in fairly defined trading ranges rather than in strongly trending markets.

Figure 1.3 shows a series of hypothetical closing prices with a 10-day momentum calculation, computed by subtracting the price 10 days earlier from the current price. This example illustrates several important momentum characteristics.

While the momentum line mirrors the general swings of the price action (the peaks and troughs of both lines coincide), important differences are evident. First, the momentum line does not mimic the broad upward price trend (although the momentum peaks are farther above the equilibrium line than the momentum troughs are below it); it does, however, underscore the shorter-term price swings or trends. Second, momentum at

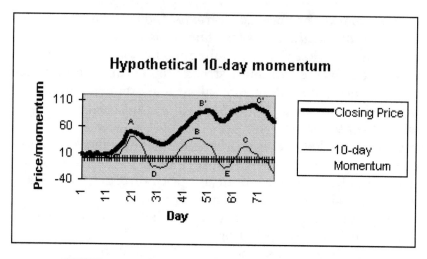

**FIGURE 1.3**    Price with a 10-Day Momentum Calculation

times appears to change direction ahead of price—its important leading characteristic. Both price and momentum reverse at roughly the same time at the conclusion of the first major upswing at point *A*. After price and momentum both reverse to the downside, a second up move commences. This time, however, the momentum peak at point *B* occurs *before* the corresponding price peak at point *B'*, and momentum has, in fact, begun to noticeably diminish—flatten out—while this leg of the uptrend is still in full force. Again, comparing points *C* and *C'*, it is evident that momentum peaks earlier than price. For momentum to continue to advance or decline, price gains or losses must continue to increase in size. If prices rise or fall at a constant rate, the momentum line will be flat; if price increases or decreases at a slower rate, momentum will reverse. Falling momentum can, for example, accompany rising prices in an uptrend. (Momentum—change in price—is the first difference, or derivative, of price. The second derivative is the change in the change of price, referred to as *acceleration.* When a price series moves from 20 to 22 to 24, momentum is steady at 2 points per day and is exhibiting no acceleration; when prices moves from 20 to 22 to 25 to 32, both momentum and acceleration are increasing.) Also note that momentum equilibrium line crossings function as general trend signals. When the momentum line reaches the equilibrium level in this example, the current price is equal to the price 10 days earlier.

Another important point is the relationship between the successive price peaks at A, B', and C' and their corresponding momentum peaks. The long-term price uptrend is countered by a general downward slope in the momentum peaks. When price makes successive higher highs at B' and C', momentum actually makes successive *lower* highs at points B and C, suggesting that while price is pushing to higher levels, it is doing so with weaker momentum—behavior that signals a trend running out of steam and a possible directional change. This phenomenon is called *divergence* because the price action and the indicator are moving in opposite directions; the indicator fails to confirm higher highs or lower lows in price. Divergence is one of the most important characteristics of momentum studies. (And as will be evident later, it is also one of the more difficult signals to interpret.)

The final characteristic to note is how important the issue of trend is when working with momentum. The momentum peaks at points A, B, and C did in fact accompany price downturns. However, the first two of these moves at any rate were revealed to be temporary corrections in a longer-term uptrend. The potential profit of selling these relatively overbought levels must be weighed against the potential profit of participating on the long side of the longer-term uptrend. The oversold levels at points D and E, however, were much less extreme than their overbought counterparts, although they represented much more desirable trading points.

A strongly trending market that accelerates into a top or bottom, however, may present a much different picture. Dynamic shorter- to intermediate-length trends may not exhibit much momentum decay. Figure 1.4 provides an example of such a situation. The market accelerates strongly into its peak (after a brief price pause and slight momentum downturn), matched by a momentum spike. (Note: Momentum indicators

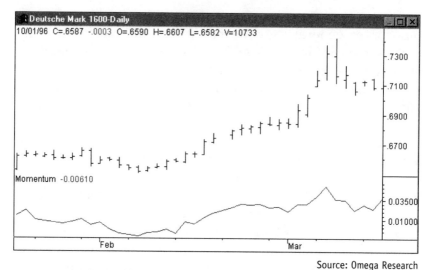

**FIGURE 1.4**   Simultaneous Price and Momentum Peaks

are usually plotted below a price chart for easy visual analysis and alignment of peaks and troughs. Depending on the indicator, these studies take the form of lines or histograms. Figure 1.5 shows 10-day momentum plotted in both formats for comparison.)

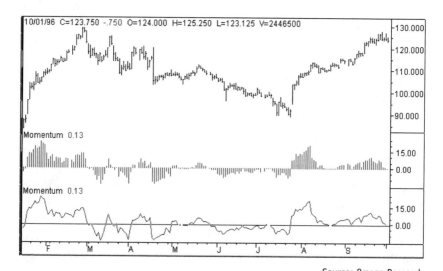

Source: Omega Research

**FIGURE 1.5**   Ten-Day Momentum in both Line and Histogram Formats

The characteristics illustrated in the earlier hypothetical example are common to virtually all oscillators and form the basis of their importance in price analysis and technical trading. Despite the variety of names and myriad formulas, most momentum indicators are variations on a few major themes. The next chapter will look more closely at how the concepts in this chapter are reflected in several calculations that form the basis of most oscillators.

# 2

# MOMENTUM OSCILLATORS: BASIC CONSTRUCTION AND COMPONENTS

Although momentum oscillators can function as trend indicators, they are more commonly used to measure the rate of price change and highlight overextended or exhausted price moves. There are several ways to measure this aspect of price behavior. (It should be noted that some traders apply the term *oscillator* only to specific momentum indicators, like the relative strength index (RSI) and stochastic studies, that share specific traits like a normalized $y$ axis scale. However, in this text the term will be used as a general one to describe all those indicators that display price change in a similar fashion to that described in Chapter 1.) Any calculation that measures the rate at which prices are changing can function as the basis for a momentum indicator.

As shown, the basic momentum calculation is the difference between the current price and a past price. A virtually equivalent calculation is to divide the current price by the past price; this merely expresses momentum as the ratio of two prices rather than the difference. Alternate methods include taking the difference between price and a moving average, or the difference between two moving averages of different lengths (sometimes referred to as a *price oscillator,* or *dual moving average* [DMA] oscillator). The more rapidly price rises or falls, the farther away price will stray from the moving average (or a short-term moving average will stray from a longer-term moving average). Oscillators constructed in this fashion are also referred to as trend deviation indicators because they show how far price moves from a mean price, or trend, represented by a moving average. Like the simple momentum formula, equivalent indicators can be constructed by division rather than subtraction—for instance, dividing price by a moving average or dividing a short-term moving average by a long-term moving average instead of calculating the differences between these entities. Although these formulas have different $y$-axis scales, they all share the basic function of measuring the speed with which prices increase or decrease.

For example, Figure 2.1 shows the daily prices for American Airlines with a 20-day moving average. At the bottom of the chart is an oscillator that plots the difference between the price and the moving average: $P_t - MA_t$, where $P_t$ is today's (closing) price and $MA_t$ is today's 20-day moving average value. The effect is equivalent to pulling the moving average into a straight line and using it as the equilibrium line of the oscillator. When price is above the moving average, the oscillator value is positive; when price is below the moving average, the oscillator value is negative. When prices are moving very quickly, that is, exhibiting strong momentum, they move farther away from the moving average and accordingly register a more extreme high or low oscillator reading. Note also that the indicator functions as a basic trend-identification tool: When the oscillator is positive, prices are above their 20-day average; when the oscillator is negative, prices are below the 20-day average.

Similarly, an oscillator built with two moving averages measures momentum by showing how far the shorter moving

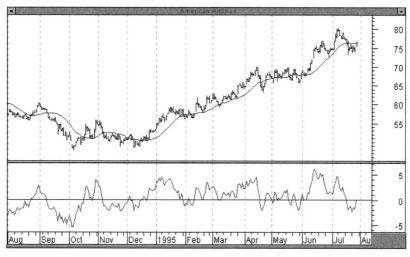

Source: Equis International

**FIGURE 2.1**   Price with a 20-Day Moving Average and a Price-Moving Average Oscillator

average (which more closely tracks short-term price fluctuations) strays from the longer moving average (which becomes the median line of the oscillator) using the formula $MA_S - MA_L$, where $MA_S$ is the shorter moving average and $MA_L$ is the longer moving average.

Again, these oscillators can be alternately constructed using division instead of subtraction. In the first case, the current closing price would be divided by the moving average value $(P_t/MA_t)$; in the second case, the shorter-term average would be divided by the longer-term moving average $(MA_S/MA_L)$. Variations on the basic calculations exist, as shown in the price oscillator description in Chapter 9.

Figure 2.2 compares three simple momentum studies based on some of the previously discussed concepts: The first (at top) is the basic momentum calculation—the current closing price minus the closing price 10 days earlier; the second is a price oscillator constructed by subtracting a 10-day moving average from a 5-day moving average; and the third (at bottom, below the price series) is an oscillator constructed by subtracting a 10-day moving average from the current closing

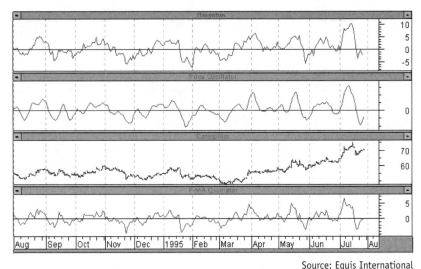

Source: Equis International

**FIGURE 2.2**    Comparison of Three Simple Momentum Studies

price. After first noting the similarities of these studies and the way they follow the swings of the market, we can use them to begin to discuss some of the common elements and issues of oscillators: the equilibrium line, the relationship of period length and amplitude, and overbought and oversold levels.

## EQUILIBRIUM LINES

Each of the three oscillators in Figure 2.2 has a horizontal median, or equilibrium line (the "zero line"), representing neutral momentum that separates positive values from negative values. In the case of the first oscillator $(P_t - P_{t-n})$, this line represents a closing price equal to the closing price 10 days earlier. For the second oscillator $(MA_S - MA_L)$, the zero line represents a 5-day moving average value equal to the 10-day moving average value. For the third oscillator $(P_t - MA_t)$, the zero line represents a closing price equal to the 10-day moving average value. When momentum is positive and moving away from the zero line, prices are rising at an increasing rate; when momentum is negative and moving away from the zero line, prices are falling at an increasing rate. The farther the momentum reading is from the zero line, the more extended the price move.

Equilibrium lines play a crucial role in the often-overlooked oscillator function of identifying trend direction. When momentum crosses the equilibrium line, a directional change is signaled, the significance of which is related to the indicator length: A zero line crossing by a 40-day momentum indicator, for example, implies a greater shift than a crossing by a 10-day indicator. Figure 2.3 illustrates this, as well as the higher number of false signals, or whipsaws, the shorter indicator produces as it moves above and below the zero line. In the case of an oscillator constructed by comparing two moving averages, a zero line crossing represents a phenomenon familiar to most technical traders: the moving average crossover, a traditional trend-following signal. When the oscillator moves above the zero line, it means the shorter moving average has moved above the longer moving average, and vice-versa. In the price-moving average oscillator, a zero line crossing represents price moving above or below its average, another basic trend signal.

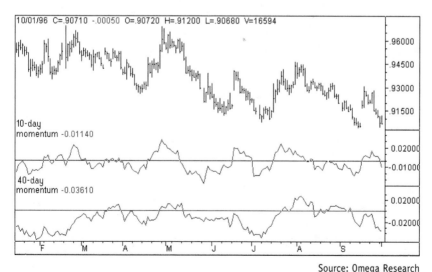

Source: Omega Research

**FIGURE 2.3**   Equilibrium Line Crossings in 10- and 40-Day Momentum Studies

## PERIOD LENGTH

The number of days (or minutes, hours, weeks, or months) used in a study determines how closely the indicator follows the market. Oscillators filter out trends longer than the length of the indicator. As with moving averages, a shorter period length creates a more sensitive, noisier oscillator (with a smaller amplitude) that highlights shorter-term price moves, whereas a longer period creates a less noisy oscillator (with a larger amplitude) that ignores shorter-term fluctuations. (However, with some smoothed oscillators, as will be demonstrated later, the period length/amplitude relationship is reversed: Shorter-term studies have a larger amplitude than longer-term studies.) Figure 2.4 compares 5-, 14-, and 40-day momentum studies (from top to bottom). The 5-day study is more erratic than either of the longer studies; the 40-day indicator mostly follows the broader turns of the market. Also note the difference in the scales of the three studies: The amplitude (in absolute points) of the 40-day oscillator is larger than that of the shorter-period oscillators.

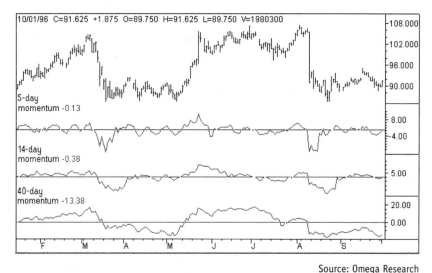

Source: Omega Research

**FIGURE 2.4**  Comparison of 5-, 14-, and 40-Day Momentum Studies

Many popular momentum indicators have become associated with particular period lengths over the years—the 14-day RSI, for example. The logic behind these periods varies. In the case of the RSI, Welles Wilder, the indicator's developer, selected 14 days because it represented half the natural 28-day monthly (lunar) cycle. However, the roughly monthlong period he based his indicator on consists of 28 *calendar* days, but only 20 *trading* days. There is no evidence to suggest a particular time period is best for all indicators or markets, or even a single indicator in a single market for an extended period of time. In practice, the number of periods will vary depending on the time frame the trader wishes to monitor and his or her trading goals. Also, the length of the study dictates the placement of overbought and oversold extremes: The more volatile the momentum study, the farther away from the equilibrium line the extreme zones will be placed. Commonly referenced indicator lengths should be considered starting points for a trader's own research and experimentation. However, extremely short (e.g., one day) or long (e.g., 60 days) period lengths generally make poor candidates for momentum-based indicators. A very short-term study will be too noisy to interpret; a very long-term study will be overwhelmed by trend.

Some noise can be removed from shorter momentum studies through the application of a moving average to smooth the data. As with any smoothing technique, the benefits of reduced noise must be weighed against the introduction of lag inherent in moving averages. Some traders believe unsmoothed momentum indicators are more useful because they are better at highlighting short-term momentum extremes. And as will be shown later, combining the unique properties of momentum indicators and moving averages can produce very interesting trading tools.

## OVERBOUGHT AND OVERSOLD

The momentum studies we have examined so far are unbounded indicators: There are no absolute highs or lows or fixed overbought or oversold levels (other than the daily price limit enforced by the exchange for a particular trading instrument) as is common with many of the bounded, or normalized, oscillators that fluctuate between set extremes.

Overbought and oversold levels represent extreme oscillator readings—points where price may be overextended and poised for correction. Because identifying price extremes is one of the fundamental functions of the momentum oscillator, a reasonable question is what constitutes "overbought" or "oversold." A simple method of determination is to establish extreme zones visually by surveying past price activity and the corresponding oscillator peaks and troughs, and selecting levels that exclude most of the oscillator readings—enough that oscillator values that move beyond these levels can reasonably be called extreme. (Though this may seem vague and subjective now, this issue will be dealt with in greater detail in subsequent chapters.) Traders commonly try to set zones that isolate the upper and lower 10 percent of oscillator values. Normalized oscillators like the RSI and stochastic studies fluctuate between fixed upper and lower boundaries, making the establishment of symmetrical overbought and oversold levels easier. The RSI, for example, fluctuates between 0 and 100, with an equilibrium line value of 50; default overbought and oversold levels for a 14-period RSI are typically set at 70 and 30, respectively—equidistant from the upper and lower boundaries.

## OSCILLATORS: BASIC INTERPRETATIONS AND APPLICATIONS

A review of some of the basic momentum characteristics and the different ways momentum oscillators can be constructed touches upon many of these indicators' common trading applications. Figure 2.5 depicts a typical normalized oscillator—probably the most widely used type of momentum study—containing the momentum line (as well as a moving average of that line), the absolute upper and lower boundaries, midpoint, and overbought and oversold zones. Here, we'll outline

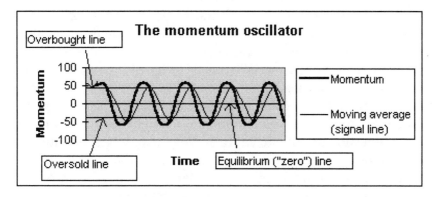

**FIGURE 2.5**   A Typical Normalized Oscillator

the different ways the information the oscillator provides can be used to trade.

## Overbought and Oversold Levels

Determining when price is overextended is one of the most important functions (along with registering divergences and indicating trend) of the momentum oscillator. Extreme momentum readings identify *potential* price exhaustion areas. These overbought and oversold levels are usually drawn as horizontal lines equidistant from the upper and lower boundaries as shown in Figure 2.5. A move by the oscillator above or below these levels signifies an extreme move.

Some of the complexities of establishing overbought and oversold levels and interpreting extreme oscillator readings are logically defining what constitutes overbought or oversold and accounting for trend influence. In a strong uptrend, for example, oscillator values tend to remain high, giving many (false) overbought signals but few, if any, oversold signals. In a rally, the latter would be much more valuable for traders looking for places to enter the existing trend. To compensate for this effect, one or both of the extreme levels can be adjusted—in this case, moving the oversold line higher (closer to the equilibrium line) to capture more of the oscillator troughs, and/or moving the overbought line higher (farther away from the equilibrium line) to exclude more of the oscillator peaks. As mentioned earlier, indicator length also impacts the placement of overbought/oversold levels. Figure 2.6 shows overbought/oversold lines adjusted to a strong uptrend. This, however, is an extreme (and idealized) example. The lines were set visually, and the oversold threshold had to be moved almost to the equilibrium line to capture dips. Also, it was possible to determine levels in retrospect; establishing such levels in real time presents a much greater challenge because it's impossible to know how long or how strong a trend will be.

The traditional interpretation of overbought/oversold levels is to sell when momentum moves above the overbought line and buy when momentum moves below the oversold line. An important issue here concerns the precise timing of the trade. A trade could be executed based on several events: when momentum first penetrates the extreme zone, when it reverses by a certain amount after entering the extreme zone, when it subsequently exits the extreme zone—*or only upon confirmation by a price signal*. Subsequent chapters will cover these issues in detail.

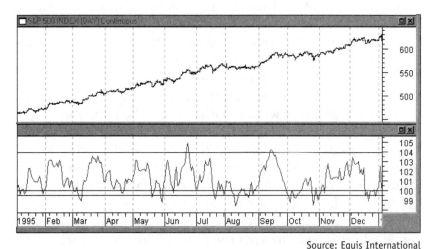

Source: Equis International

**FIGURE 2.6**    Overbought/Oversold Lines Adjusted to a Strong Uptrend

## Divergence

Another fundamental oscillator application is to look for *divergence* between momentum and price—when price moves in one direction while momentum moves in the opposite direction. This characteristic—the tendency of momentum to dissipate as a trend nears conclusion—was already discussed in Chapter 1. Price may continue to rise or fall, but if momentum fails to confirm the move by doing likewise, it may be advance warning of a correction or trend change.

The term *divergence* is most frequently used to describe the specific circumstance of price making a higher high or lower low that is not confirmed by momentum—the oscillator instead makes a lower high or a higher low, respectively. Figure 2.7 illustrates this concept. Price makes a new high, but the corresponding momentum peak is actually lower than its preceding peak, suggesting that price has pushed to its new level on weaker momentum and the trend might be vulnerable. A correction did, in fact, follow. This pattern, at price tops and bottoms, is known as a *classic* divergence. When it occurs

Source: Omega Research

**FIGURE 2.7**    Classic Bearish Divergence

at a price top, it is also referred to as a *bearish* divergence because it portends a downside reversal (as in this case); at a market bottom it is called a *bullish* divergence. By warning of a potential trend change, such signals can allow the trader to liquidate existing positions (or perhaps move a protective stop closer) or establish new ones in anticipation of a new trend.

Markets do not always post single divergences as shown in this example. Especially in strongly trending markets, several divergences may occur as the market makes successive price peaks or troughs, giving multiple false signals before the market actually reverses.

## Equilibrium Line Crossings

Because momentum oscillators are smoothed representations of price action, equilibrium line crossings, as discussed earlier, represent a directional movement shift (more or less so depending on the period length) and can be used to place trend-following trades. Long trades are entered when the momentum line crosses above the equilibrium line and sells when the momentum line crosses below it. Although price oscillators (shorter-term moving average – longer-term moving average) are simply alternate representations of moving average crossovers, there are advantages to displaying them in oscillator form: Patterns are much easier to see, and it is easier to anticipate crossovers and divergences.[1]

Like other trend-following approaches, equilibrium line crossovers are subject to whipsaws in choppy or congested markets. To filter some of these false signals, a buffer zone or band can be placed around the zero line. This zone requires momentum to move a certain amount above or below it before a trade can be executed.

## Patterns and Trend Analysis

Another way to use momentum is to apply familiar price-based techniques like chart patterns (head and shoulders formations, support and resistance, etc.) and trendlines. Because of the leading characteristic of momentum, analyzing such activity in the momentum series rather than the price series can provide more timely signals (at the risk of early or false signals). However, the interpretation of techniques like chart patterns is as subjective on momentum data as it is on price data. As a result, this book will focus more on the mathematically definable aspects of oscillators.

Trend-following techniques like moving averages can also be applied to momentum studies. Several widely followed studies incorporate moving averages in the form of *signal lines*—when the momentum study crosses above or below its moving average, a directional change is implied. A change in momentum, in turn, implies a potential price change. And again, because of momentum lead, these points present opportunities to get in early on a price move. Such crossovers are commonly used as entry or exit triggers. For example, an oscillator that uses a moving average signal line may move into its overbought zone; a sell is triggered when the indicator peaks and then crosses below its signal line (refer to Figure 2.5).

The various momentum oscillator signals can be used in a number of ways—first, to enter trades, either from a trend-following standpoint using equilibrium line crossings, or in anticipation of a reversal from overbought or oversold signals. The latter signals also offer exit points for existing trades. A trader might choose to liquidate all or part of a long position when the indicator moves above a particular overbought threshold, for example. Alternately, if a trader's strategy incorporated a *trailing stop,* a move into the extreme zone could require that the stop be moved closer to the market to protect against a potential reversal.

## SUMMARY

Having discussed the basic momentum concept, this chapter has summarized some of the different ways it can be calculated. Despite the variety of formulas, the end results are very similar—all momentum indicators share a handful of critical elements. To offer a better understanding of the basic applications of these indicators and the challenges of trading with them, the next chapter will look closely at several widely used oscillators and will examine the usefulness of these tools in different market situations. Subsequent chapters will offer more detail about some of the topics touched on in this chapter, including divergence, defining overbought and oversold levels, and selecting period lengths.

# 3

## POPULAR MOMENTUM INDICATORS

Anyone who even casually studies technical analysis soon becomes aware of the great popularity of momentum oscillators. The studies in this chapter are found in virtually every charting and analysis software program and are referenced in almost every trading book and manual. As the best-known examples of momentum indicators, they provide an excellent foundation on which to begin investigating oscillator-based trading strategies. In this chapter an overview of these tools will outline their construction and highlight their distinguishing characteristics and standard applications. Then, the next chapter will take a closer look at the performance of some simple trade signals associated with some of these indicators.

For simplicity's sake, all the calculations are described using daily data. However, weekly, monthly, or hourly, data can be substituted. *Price,* unless otherwise noted, refers to the closing price of a daily price bar.

## MOMENTUM AND RATE OF CHANGE

### Background

Though momentum is used as a generic term to describe the broad concept of the speed with which prices change, it is also the name of a particular technical study. This indicator was already discussed in some detail in Chapter 1. Although the terms *momentum* and *rate of change* (ROC) are sometimes used interchangeably, the former usually refers to the difference between the current price and a past price and the latter to the ratio between the current price and a past price. The resultant indicators, however, are virtually identical except for their scales. These fundamental tools are the most straightforward and easy-to-understand examples of the momentum indicator.

### Calculation

The momentum calculation shows the price difference between the current price and a price $n$ days earlier:

Momentum = Price (today) − price ($n$ days ago), so

Momentum = $P_t - P_{t-n}$

where
$P_t$ = current price
$P_{t-n}$ = Price $n$ days earlier.

The median, or equilibrium, line of the momentum calculation is zero; momentum crosses this boundary whenever the current price rises above or falls below the price $n$ days earlier.

The ROC calculation *divides* the current price by the price $n$ days earlier:

$$ROC = \frac{\text{Price (today)}}{\text{price (}n\text{ days ago)}}, \text{ so}$$

$$\text{ROC} = \frac{P_t}{P_{t-n}}$$

Some software programs multiply this formula by 100:

$$\text{ROC} = 100 * \left(\frac{P_t}{P_{t-n}}\right)$$

In the first ROC calculation, the equilibrium line has a value of 1 (one). In the second calculation, the equilibrium line value is 100; a momentum reading at this line means the current price is the same as—that is, 100 percent of—the price $n$ days earlier.

Figure 3.1 plots both a 20-day ROC and a 20-day momentum study and shows that the calculations are basically indistinguishable. An alternate version of the ROC calculation, sometimes referred to as *price rate of change,* divides the change in price over an $n$-day period by the closing price $n$ days ago: $(P_t - P_{t-n})/P_{t-n}$. In other words, if the price change over the last five days was 10 points and the closing price five days ago was 50, the price rate of change would be $10/50 = .20$. This variation combines elements of both the momentum

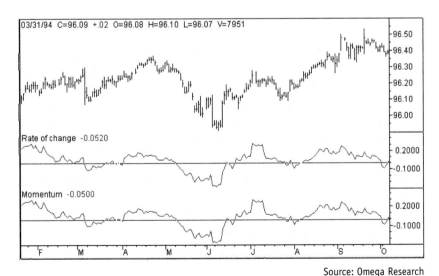

Source: Omega Research

**FIGURE 3.1**   Twenty-Day ROC and 20-Day Momentum Studies

and basic ROC calculations—the price differential (momentum) over a given period is compared to the price at the beginning of the lookback period and expressed as a ratio (like the ROC formula). The result, however, is still the same.

## Logic

The basic momentum principles outlined in Chapter 1 are exemplified by these indicators. Day-to-day (or hour-to-hour, week-to-week, etc.) price change in strongly trending markets tends to increase, or accelerate, whereas it tends to remain constant, or decrease, in congested markets or as trends run out of steam. Extremely high or low momentum readings alert the trader to potentially exhausted price moves. Zero line crossings signal trend changes, the magnitude of which depend on the period length of the study; longer indicators reflect longer-term trends. As a result, these tools (like most momentum indicators) have both trend-following and countertrend applications: to identify longer-term trend direction as well as shorter-term swing points suitable for profit-taking or reentry into existing trends.

## Distinguishing Characteristics

Despite their simplicity, momentum and ROC convey much of the same information as their more complex oscillator cousins: They display directional movement, extreme momentum levels, and divergence. In their basic form, they are unbounded, unsmoothed measures of price change—they do not have finite upper and lower boundaries or standardized overbought/oversold levels. Indicator readings are technically unlimited (daily price limits provide the only real boundary), so extreme levels can be established either on a visual basis, that is, drawing lines that exclude a suitable percentage of the indicator values, or by using a statistical technique that identifies high and low extremes (this method will be outlined fully in Chapter 6).

The momentum calculation $(P_t - P_{t-n})$ can be normalized by expressing it in terms of the maximum possible price range over a given time period. Simply divide the day's momentum value by the daily price limit multiplied by the number of days in the indicator:

$$\text{Normalized Momentum } (M_n) = \frac{M_t}{(D * P)},$$

where
$M_t$ = today's original momentum reading
$D$ = daily price limit for a given market
$P$ = period length

For example, a 10-day momentum value would be divided by 10 times the daily price limit for that market. The result can then be multiplied by a constant to create a desired scale.

One important characteristic of a standard, unsmoothed momentum or ROC calculation is the sometimes troublesome effect of data drop-off, which can cause dramatic and misleading momentum readings when old prices disappear as the indicator time window moves forward. For example, if an isolated closing price is abnormally high or low compared to the recent price activity, a momentum or ROC study may show unusual movement—both when that closing price is first factored into the study and later when it drops off the back end of the calculation—even when very little change is taking place in the current price action.

Consider the 10-day momentum study shown in Table 3.1 and Figure 3.2. This example essentially consists of two horizontal trading ranges separated by a dramatic spike: On day 17 price more than triples the previous day's price of 13. Now observe the behavior of the momentum line. When price leaps to 40, momentum mirrors this behavior by spiking in its own right. In the aftermath of this abnormal leap, price settles into another trading range.

Momentum, by contrast, spikes downward on day 26 despite the trading range in effect at the time—in fact, the

**TABLE 3.1**   Ten-Day Momentum Study

| Closing Price | 10-day Momentum | Closing Price | 10-day Momentum |
|---|---|---|---|
| 18 | | 21 | 6 |
| 14 | | 19 | 2 |
| 15 | | 23 | 5 |
| 16 | | 25 | 11 |
| 15 | | 22 | 7 |
| 17 | | 23 | 10 |
| 18 | | 24 | −16 |
| 16 | | 24 | 2 |
| 18 | | 22 | 0 |
| 14 | −4 | 20 | −1 |
| 15 | 1 | 21 | 2 |
| 17 | 2 | 24 | 1 |
| 18 | 2 | 22 | −3 |
| 14 | −1 | 23 | 1 |
| 15 | −2 | 20 | −3 |
| 13 | −5 | 21 | −3 |
| 40 | 24 | 22 | −2 |
| 22 | 4 | 24 | 2 |
| 22 | 8 | 23 | 3 |

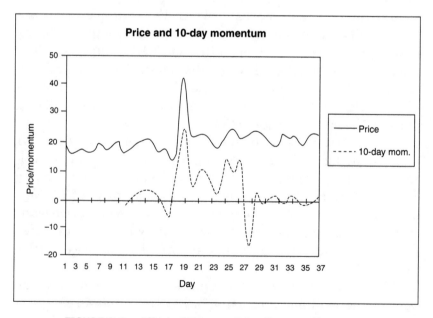

**FIGURE 3.2**   Effect of Extreme Price Move on Momentum

market on this day has posted its third consecutive (marginally) higher close. However, day 26 also marks the day the past price spike from day 17 was again factored into the 10-day momentum calculation (day 26 − day 17). Then, on day 27 momentum leaps upward (crossing back above the zero line) as the extreme price from day 17 once again drops out of the calculation. As a result, a past isolated price incident causes extreme and misleading momentum readings much later. Entering trades based on the downward zero crossing and extreme oversold reading on day 26 or the upward zero line crossing on day 27 would have been useless in light of the subsequent sideways price activity.

## Standard Applications

As previously discussed, momentum and ROC lend themselves to both trend trading and countertrend applications. Trend-following positions are entered when the indicator crosses above or below the zero line (notice how these crossings in Figure 3.1 correspond to the general market trends). Momentum and ROC extremes generate overbought/oversold trade opportunities that can be used to take profits on existing positions, reenter trending markets, or establish new positions in anticipation of a trend change; the most common interpretation is to look for a possible reversal, or at least a consolidation, when momentum reaches an extreme. Momentum and ROC also display divergences that can be used to identify potential turning points. These indicators also lend themselves well to charting techniques like trendlines and support and resistance. A break in a momentum trendline, like a reversal in an overbought or oversold momentum reading, alerts the trader to a possible price reversal. Figure 3.3 shows corresponding trendline breaks in momentum and price in the silver market. Notice that the momentum break precedes the price break. This break is itself predated by a bearish divergence between the two prominent price peaks in late July and late August: Price makes a higher high while momentum makes a lower high.

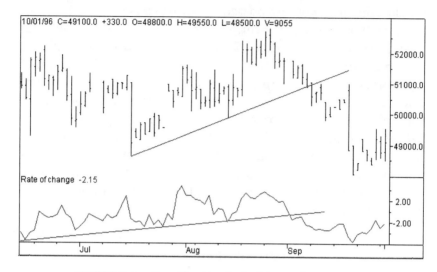

**FIGURE 3.3**   Trendline Breaks in Price and Momentum

## THE RELATIVE STRENGTH INDEX

### Background

Welles Wilder introduced the relative strength index (RSI) in his 1978 book *New Concepts in Technical Trading Systems* (Trend Research). His motivation was to correct some of the deficiencies he found in standard momentum oscillators (as described earlier), most notably:

1. They are subject to erratic readings because of extreme price swings.
2. They lack a uniform scale for the y-axis; overbought and oversold levels are thus different for every instrument.

As a result, the RSI (1) contains an internal smoothing mechanism to lessen the impact of extreme fluctuations and (2) creates a constant scale for the y-axis ranging from 0 to 100, making it theoretically possible, according to Wilder, to compare different markets as well as past price movement to current price movement for the same instrument. Wilder's RSI should not be confused with relative strength, which compares one instrument to another or to a benchmark—for example, comparing an individual stock to the Dow Jones Industrial Average.

## Calculation

The RSI calculation creates a momentum oscillator by comparing the average up movement (up momentum) to the average down movement (down momentum) over a given time period. In his original writings, Wilder outlined the calculation of a 14-day RSI with overbought and oversold levels of 70 and 30.

$$RSI = 100 - \left[ \frac{100}{(1 + RS)} \right],$$

where
RS = relative strength
  = the average of the up closes over the calculation period divided by the average of the down closes over the calculation period.

The relative strength (RS) is the key calculation in the formula—it generates a smoothed momentum figure that can be adjusted by altering the number of days in the calculation. The rest of the math simply normalizes the scale of the RSI to a constant range of 0 to 100.

The RS for a 14-day period is calculated by dividing the 14-day up close average by the 14-day down close average. *Up closes* and *down closes* refer to the absolute change in price from close to close (a one-day momentum calculation). For example, if today's close is higher than yesterday's close, today is an up day, and the difference between the two closes becomes the up close amount for the day. If today's close is lower than yesterday's close, today is a down day, and the absolute value of the difference of the closes becomes today's down day figure. If a 14-day period contains eight up closes and six down closes, the gains for the eight up days are summed and divided by 14, as are the losses for the six down days (again, the absolute values of the down day figures are used—not negative numbers). In effect, the up close value for a day that closed lower than the previous day is zero, and vice versa. RS is the average up close figure divided by the average down close figure; it is plugged into the preceding formula to generate the RSI.

Wilder used an additional smoothing method to simplify continued RSI calculations after the initial period. After computing the first 14-day figure, the RS for each successive day is calculated by multiplying the previous day's average up close by the number of days in the calculation period minus one, adding the current day's up close value, and then dividing the result by the number of days in the calculation period. The same procedure is performed for down days. For a 14-day period, for example, one would multiply yesterday's up close average by 13, add the current day's up close value, and divide the result by 14; the process would be repeated for the down day figures. The resulting smoothed RS figure is used in the RSI formula. Most programs use this or a similar exponential smoothing technique.

## Logic

The RSI embodies the same principles as momentum and ROC—it is an average momentum measurement. In essence, the RSI measures momentum by creating a constantly smoothed ratio—the relative strength—of price advances versus price declines (in the form of one-day momentum) over a given time period. While the RSI calculation normalizes the indicator's readings, overbought and oversold levels are not truly comparable between markets, or between different phases in the same market.

## Distinguishing Characteristics

The most important innovations in the RSI are, in fact, its internal smoothing and normalized range. The averaged momentum and smoothing calculations alleviate some of the impact of extreme price swings. The normalized 0 to 100 scale provides a benchmark for overbought and oversold levels. The equilibrium level is 50, and is equivalent to the zero line of the momentum calculation. The standard extreme zones for the 14-day RSI are 70 and 30, respectively. Prices above or below these levels are considered overextended, and indicate the possibility of a trend change or consolidation.

Because of its smoothing, the RSI often resembles a slightly flattened or more "compact" momentum or ROC study. Figure 3.4 compares 10-day RSI and ROC studies. Though the indicators are very similar, there are a few differences: In the price jump in July (and the subsequent trading range) the ROC indicator makes a fairly large top; the RSI moves up and then forms a gradual divergence pattern, slowly trending down while price inches up. Unlike momentum or ROC, however, the amplitude of the RSI wave *decreases* as the period length increases because of the indicator's smoothing factor; a 10-day RSI will swing higher and lower than a 20-day RSI (see Figure 3.5).

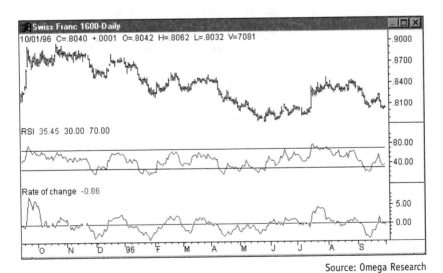

Source: Omega Research

**FIGURE 3.4**  Comparison of 10-Day RSI and ROC Studies

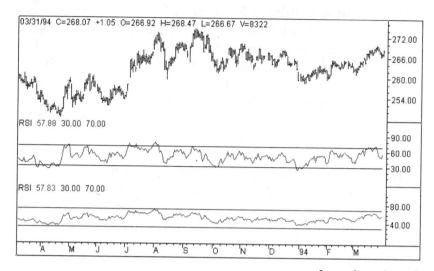

Source: Omega Research
**FIGURE 3.5**    Comparison of 10-Day and 20-Day RSIs

## Standard Applications

In his book, Wilder summarized several RSI applications, including overbought/oversold readings, divergences (singled out as the RSI's "most indicative characteristic"), chart formations and support/resistance (which he said were sometimes evident in the RSI but not in price), and failure swings. For our purposes, the first two applications are the most important. Like momentum, ROC, and other oscillators, these patterns can be used to establish new positions or take profits on existing ones.

Referring again to Figure 3.4, the similarity between the RSI and ROC is apparent—aside from the obvious scale differences, the lines have a great deal in common. Not surprisingly, the RSI can be used as a trend indicator as well—crossings of the equilibrium line (50) can be interpreted much the same as zero line crossings in momentum or ROC studies. Overbought/oversold RSI values correspond to several turning points in the market (but note the greater frequency of oversold signals because of the downtrend prevalent over much of the example). There is also divergence between the higher price high in October 1995 and the lower RSI high (this pattern occurs in the ROC as well).

## STOCHASTICS (%K/%D)

### Background

The stochastic oscillator, like the RSI, is a smoothed, normalized momentum indicator with set lower and upper boundaries of 0 and 100. (The term *stochastic* came about as something of an accident; stochastic theory actually involves the study of random motion.) Popularized by George Lane, stochastics consists of two lines: %K, which measures the relative position of the current close within a price range defined by the user, and %D, a three-day average of the %K line that functions as a signal line. When %K crosses above or below %D, a market turn is implied.

### Calculation

Stochastics measures momentum by comparing the recent close to the absolute price range (high of the range − low of the range) over an *n*-day period. For example, for a 10-day stochastic, the difference between today's close and the lowest low of the last 10 days would be divided by the difference between the highest high and the lowest low of the last 10 days; the result would then be multiplied by 100. The formula for the first line, %K, is:

$$\%K = 100 * \left( \frac{C_t - L_n}{H_n - L_n} \right),$$

where
$C_t$ is today's closing price
$H_n$ is the highest price of the last $n$ days
$L_n$ is the lowest price of the last $n$ days

$\%D$ = a three-period moving average of %K
      = average (%K,3)

Because of the noisiness of the raw %K and %D lines (commonly calculated over a five-day period and referred to as *fast stochastics*), an additionally smoothed version of stochastics called *slow stochastics* is usually used by software programs and is most frequently referred to simply as stochastics. The original %D line becomes the new slow %K line; in turn, this line is smoothed with a three-day moving average to create the new slow %D line. (However, Lane thinks the quicker version is actually more useful for *experienced* traders.) Figure 3.6 shows both fast and slow ten-day stochastic studies in the S&P 500. The additional smoothing of the slow version results in fewer %K/%D whipsaws, as well as slower indicator response.

## Logic

Stochastics is based on the supposed tendency of price to close in the direction of the trend—that is, closing toward the upper end of the price bar in bull moves and toward the lower end of the price bar in bear moves. However, this characteristic is not a universal or reliable facet of price behavior, although it

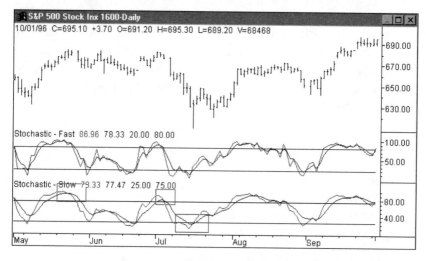

Source: Omega Research

**FIGURE 3.6**   Fast and Slow 10-Day Stochastic Studies

is sometimes observable in a shorter series of dynamically up- or down-trending bars. Conversely, price sometimes closes at the opposite end of the price bar at market turning points, especially at extremes like spike highs or lows (for example, at the low end of a bar at a price top, the so-called key reversal pattern). More important than these issues, though, is the fact that the numerator of the stochastic equation ($\text{close}_t - \text{low}_n$) is very similar to the basic momentum formula ($\text{Price}_t - \text{Price}_n$). The denominator simply puts this fundamental momentum calculation in the context of the price range of the indicator's lookback period. Stochastics, therefore, is closely related to the other indicators we have discussed.

## Distinguishing Characteristics

The smoothed construction of the slow stochastic makes it a very visually appealing indicator; it is usually less noisy than other momentum indicators of equal length. Figure 3.7 compares the 10-day slow stochastic with the 10-day RSI and 10-day ROC (note, however, the greater similarity between the

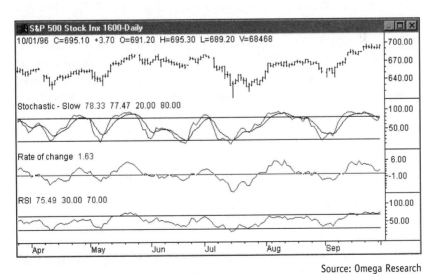

Source: Omega Research

**FIGURE 3.7**  Comparison of 10-Day Slow Stochastic with 10-Day RSI and 10-Day ROC

[fast] %K stochastic line and the RSI and ROC). Like the RSI, stochastics is a bounded study, fluctuating between 0 and 100; standard overbought and oversold levels are 80 and 20 or 70 and 30. The default period length is five days (with a three-day secondary smoothing for the slow stochastic), although longer time periods (10, 14, and 20 days) are commonly used. The presence of the second line—the %D signal line—also distinguishes stochastics from momentum, ROC, and RSI.

## Standard Applications

Although Lane has described numerous patterns and uses of the stochastic indicator, he stresses the importance of divergence—specifically divergence between price and the %D line—as the most important signal. Like the RSI, the normalized format of stochastics provides a constant band for comparison of overbought/oversold levels. Because of its smoothed composition, it does not lend itself as easily to charting techniques like trendlines as the RSI or momentum/ROC studies.

Besides basic overbought/oversold signals and divergences, penetration of the %D line by the %K line—while both are in one of the extreme zones—represents another important trading signal (see the rectangles on the slow stochastic in Figure 3.6). Lane stresses that stochastics is *not* a mechanical system, suggesting it be combined with charting techniques, cycles, and Elliott waves. Although not frequently mentioned, stochastic equilibrium line (50) crossings reflect trend changes, as with momentum, ROC, and RSI.

## MOVING AVERAGE CONVERGENCE-DIVERGENCE

### Background

Developed by Gerald Appel, moving average convergence-divergence (MACD) plots the difference of two exponential moving averages (EMAs) along with a nine-period exponential moving average of this difference as a signal line. The result is a smoothed, boundless oscillator that can signal trades via zero line crossings, divergences, signal line crossovers, and overbought and oversold conditions. Convergence-divergence simply refers to the process of the moving averages coming closer together (converging) or moving farther apart (diverging) depending on the changes in price direction and speed. The MACD has achieved great popularity because of its flexibility as both a trend-following and a countertrend tool.

## Calculation

The MACD creates a momentum oscillator by taking the difference of two exponential moving averages. (Appel's original design called for 8-day and 17-day moving averages for the "buy side" MACD, and 12- and 26-day moving averages for the "sell side" MACD; the 12- and 26-day periods are usually the default values for both sides of the market.) An additional 9-day EMA is applied to the oscillator to provide a signal line. As a result, the default indicator is often referred to as the *12–26–9 MACD*.

$$MACD = EMA_1 - EMA_2,$$

where
$EMA_1 =$    first exponential moving average period (standard setting of 12 days)
$EMA_2 =$    second exponential moving average period (standard setting of 26 days)

$$Signal\ line = EMA_3\ of\ MACD,$$

where
$EMA_3 =$    the exponential moving average period for the signal line (standard setting of 9 days).

## Logic

The fundamental momentum calculation of the MACD—the difference between two moving averages—is one that was discussed in Chapter 1. Like a standard price oscillator, the

MACD is an alternate representation of a moving average crossover system that highlights when the shorter moving average is moving away from the longer moving average: The faster the shorter average moves, the stronger the momentum. Equilibrium line crossings represent moving average crossovers. As with all oscillators, the farther away from the equilibrium line the indicator moves, the more extended the price move—thus, extreme momentum readings and possible turning points can be identified. Figure 3.8 compares a 12–26–9 MACD (bottom) to a price oscillator built with 12- and 26-day simple moving averages (top). The slight differences between the two are a result of the exponential and simple moving average calculations; a price oscillator constructed with exponential averages would look identical to the MACD except for the presence of the signal line.

## Distinguishing Characteristics

The MACD combines a number of trend indicator and oscillator elements. The standard 12–26–9 MACD is a longer-term

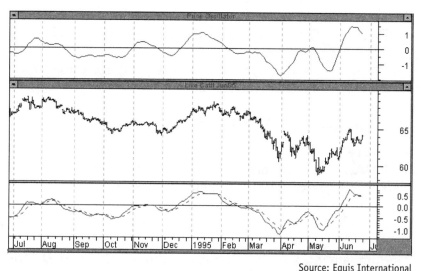

Source: Equis International

**FIGURE 3.8**  Comparison of a 12–26–9 MACD to a Price Oscillator Built with 12- and 26-Day Simple Moving Averages

indicator, and like stochastics is smoothed; as a result, it is better than most momentum studies at highlighting longer-term trends and trading opportunities. Also, like stochastics, the MACD contains a signal line that can be used to trigger trades (these signals can function as trend-following or countertrend triggers, depending on the context). The MACD has no upper or lower boundaries: Overbought and oversold levels can be set relative to past behavior. What distinguishes the MACD from a simple price oscillator is the originator's specific use of exponential moving averages, set period lengths, and proprietary applications. Like stochastics, its smoothed construction makes it more difficult to apply trendlines and other charting techniques. In addition to the indicator's two primary lines, the MACD is sometimes plotted with an additional histogram of the difference between the main line and the signal line to highlight crossovers (see Figure 3.9).

## Standard Applications

The MACD basically produces the same trading signals as the other indicators in this chapter, interpreted in a similar

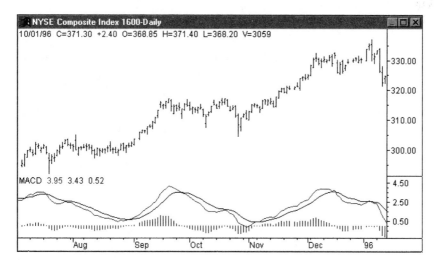

**FIGURE 3.9**  MACD Plotted with Histogram

fashion: overbought/oversold levels, divergences, and equilibrium line crossings. However, the MACD has much stronger trend-following characteristics than the other indicators. The addition of the signal line offers the opportunity to trade when the MACD crosses above or below this line—preferably when the indicator is at an extreme level. (Like other trend indicators, the MACD will produce a high number of signal line crossover whipsaws in congested and ranging markets.) Although establishing a position based on a signal line crossing when the MACD is at an extreme level may constitute a countertrend trade, this technique can also offer an opportunity to anticipate the trend changes that would be signaled by equilibrium line crossovers.

Figure 3.9 highlights some typical MACD characteristics and signals: Shorter-term price fluctuations are much less evident in the indicator; trend signals like the signal line crossovers (at relatively extreme indicator levels) and divergences (the peaks in December 1995–January 1996) indicate the more significant turning points. The additional histogram shows the difference between the MACD and its signal line; it highlights crossovers.

## SUMMARY

Having reviewed the construction, logic, and basic uses of some of the most popular momentum oscillators, the next chapter will address some of the confusion and misconceptions surrounding them and discuss some of the issues associated with applying them in the markets. It's one thing to know that an overbought reading on a momentum oscillator may signal a price downturn; it's another to act on that information.

# 4

## MOMENTUM OSCILLATORS: TRADING ISSUES

Though most traders have an intuitive grasp of what oscillators are telling them about the market, this knowledge is often superficial. A number of subtle issues make oscillator interpretation and application more complicated than first meets the eye. Momentum and oscillators present seemingly straightforward concepts: Extreme momentum readings identify market extremes and potential reversal points, as does divergence between price and momentum, and so on. But to what extent are these common interpretations reliable? How wide is the gap between analytical theory and actual trading? This chapter investigates some of the practical considerations of trading with momentum oscillators.

### BASIC CONSIDERATIONS

The attraction of momentum oscillators is not hard to understand. They contain a great deal of important market information, and they have tremendous visual impact: A single momentum indicator can define trends as well as identify shorter-term momentum extremes and divergences that frequently coincide with price reversals. Additionally, momentum often leads the market, flattening or reversing before price. Such characteristics make momentum oscillators very appealing, especially to traders who believe it's possible (and necessary) to capture virtually every market turn and suffer little, if any, drawdown. Also, one important market reality would seem to highly recommend the use of oscillators: Because markets spend far less time trending than they do wandering in trading ranges, the countertrend (or antitrend) trading possibilities of these indicators seem to offer a chance to profit in trendless markets.

Figure 4.1 illustrates these points well. The 10-day RSI follows most of the shorter-term swings of a somewhat choppy downtrend in the S&P 500 from mid-July to mid-October 1990 (although the oscillator doesn't always reach the default overbought/oversold levels of 70 and 30). The divergence between points $y$ and $z$ (marked on both the price series and the oscillator) presaged a short sideways period that eventually

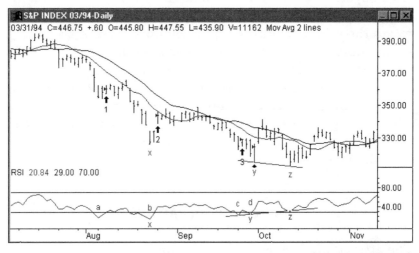

Source: Omega Research

**FIGURE 4.1**   Trading Signals in a 10-Day RSI

evolved into a healthy upside reversal (not pictured). However, upon closer inspection, certain problems with this example become apparent.

Before discussing these specifically, it's necessary to address a general problem in technical analysis. In short, the vast majority of available literature focuses overwhelmingly on trade *entry*—defining techniques that (in retrospect, at least) have a high probability of identifying reversals. The tradability, so to speak, of these points in a larger context is usually less of a concern. Generally, once a method has been defined that locates reversal points of any magnitude, the matter is usually dropped, the implication being that everything else associated with this technique—namely, the risk and where to exit—is a discretionary matter: "Here's a pattern followed by a reversal. It will get you in the market, and the market immediately moves in your favor—but you're on your own as far as getting *out* of the market and taking a profit." Trade entries, however, are only one part of the puzzle. Studies by Lebeau and Lucas in their book *Computer Analysis of the Futures Market* (1992, Business One–Irwin), for example, indicated that the majority of entry signals on their own are little or no better than random entries. Money management/risk control and exit rules are as important as, if not more important than, specific entry techniques. Although entrenched habits are, unfortunately, difficult to overcome, it's necessary for a trader to scratch a bit below the surface and take a closer look at different trade signals to see how practical they actually are. Many things that *appear* to work (especially when taken out of context), or work in isolated instances (what Jack Schwager termed "the well-chosen example"), may not prove profitable over the long haul.

Returning to the oscillator example, the oversold readings at points *a, b, c,* and *d* are accompanied by price reversals (there is actually another small penetration of the oversold line between *a* and *b,* which will be ignored for demonstration purposes). Using commonly accepted oscillator interpretation, these points represent potential buying opportunities.

However, the subsequent corrections are fairly small (in the case of point c, almost nonexistent), and before long the market resumes its trend. Two related questions arise here: First, are these reactions, considered out of context, large enough to warrant trading (taking into account commissions and slippage)? Second, in a larger market context, is it advisable to take such positions against an obvious trend?

In this example the answer to the first question is "possibly"; to the second question the answer is "probably not" (although the oversold areas might be good exit points for a trader gradually offsetting multiple short positions established at a higher price). The oversold signal at points $b$ and $d$ are followed by the largest price turnarounds, although there are no countervailing sell signals in the oscillator to take profits—a trader would need an alternate exit technique that would capture the gains of these moves before the market turns down again. Taking oscillator signals against the direction of the prevailing trend can lead to repeated losses. Also, using such signals as exit points can take a trader out of a profitable trend-following position that is still intact (note the trend direction indicated by the 10- and 20-day moving averages). One of momentum's most highly touted features, however, is its ability to reveal trend weakness and locate potential reversals with divergences; acting on such signals is by definition trading against an existing trend in anticipation of a new one. Finally, the divergence between points $y$ and $z$ was preceded by a longer-term divergence between points $x$ and $y$ and by another shorter-term divergence between the momentum extremes at $c$ and $d$.

Because the RSI produces four oversold signals and zero overbought signals during this period, relying on extreme oscillator readings to place trades would result in accumulating at least one long position (if only the first signal is acted upon), and possibly several, in a downtrending market without corresponding sell signals to take any profits or limit losses because the prevailing bear bias skews the oscillator readings in the direction of the trend. Adjusting the oscillator (or reinterpreting it) is necessary to compensate for this phenomenon.

Another consideration is when the trades can be placed. At points $a$ and $b$, for example, entering when the oscillator immediately penetrates the oversold line would result in trades that move immediately against the trader—in the case of point $b$, to a significant degree. The second method of entering the trade on the subsequent retracement of the oversold zone would mean the trader watches potential profits diminish as the market rallies before the signal is triggered. In this case, entering on an $x$- (say, two- or three-) point oscillator retracement once the indicator bottoms in the oversold zone would offer the best timing option. Also, for anyone other than a full-time trader, who can monitor real-time data and enter the market as soon as a trigger is hit, it's likely the trade would be executed on the first available close or open after the trigger, giving back additional ground on the position. Such are the potential pitfalls of shorter-term, countertrend trading with oscillators.

Casual observation indicates buying and selling on the trend signals from the moving average crossover during this period would be much more profitable (a test of both approaches over this small sample confirms this). *However, it must be noted that in a trading range environment, countertrend oscillator signals can provide much better results than trend-following signals.* Also, using a moving average or some other trend indicator to filter countertrend oscillator signals might help avoid repeated entries against a strong trend. And as noted earlier, taking signals only in the direction of the trend, in this case, would require an adjustment of the overbought zone—to nearly the level of the equilibrium line: The oscillator never reaches the overbought zone, denying entry into the trend.

As a result, a common admonition is to use oscillators in trading range markets and avoid them in trending phases. The problem with this advice, though, is that it is impossible to know when the market will switch from one mode to the other. A trader who relies on oscillator signals because a market has been fluctuating in a horizontal range for $x$ days or weeks has no certainty the market will not begin a strong trend the next day. The ability to accurately forecast when trends will begin and end would render most technical tools obsolete. One approach (which will be discussed later) might be to use a method to identify trending periods and disregard overbought/oversold oscillator signals during those periods, or only take those signals that are in the direction of the trend.

## TREND INFLUENCE

The skewing effect of trend is the primary reason a trader must exercise caution when using momentum oscillators. Although momentum indicators remove some of the directional bias from a data series (relative to the length of the study), a trend, depending on its strength, still exerts some influence on the oscillator reading, most notably in the following forms.

### Prolonged Extreme Readings

Oscillators will register sustained readings above or below their overbought or oversold levels during a long-term trend. For example, in an uptrend, a 10-period stochastic may move above an overbought level of 70 or 80 and remain there for an extended period of time, as shown in the weekly chart of the S&P 500 in Figure 4.2.

### Absence of Corresponding Oscillator Signals in the Opposite Direction of the Trend

The counterpart of the situation just described is the failure of momentum studies to generate oversold readings in bull moves and overbought readings in bear moves. Referring again to Figure 4.2, the strong uptrending period produces no oversold readings in the oscillator; the same trend force that keeps the oscillator's highs above the overbought zone also keeps the oscillator's troughs above the oversold zone. However, these would be precisely the most useful trade signals because they would allow the trader to enter or reenter the

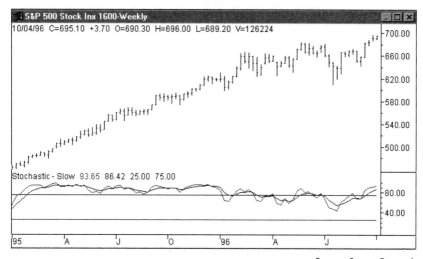

S&P 500 Stock Inx 1600-Weekly

10/04/96 C=695.10 +3.70 O=690.30 H=696.00 L=689.20 V=126224

Stochastic - Slow  93.65  86.42  25.00  75.00

Source: Omega Research

**FIGURE 4.2**    S&P 500 Uptrend with Prolonged Overbought Reading

market in the direction of the trend. Adjusting one or both of the oscillator extreme levels—for example, raising the oversold line in a strong uptrend—is necessary to compensate for this effect. Shortening the period length will also filter out more of the trend and highlight countertrend swings.

## Repeated False Divergence Signals

A series of price peaks in a long uptrend or price troughs in a long downtrend will frequently produce a string of divergences—each one *potentially* signaling a reversal, and each turning out to be merely a pause or minor correction in the dominant trend. Figure 4.3 shows several successive price peaks accompanied by classic bearish divergence signals in the ROC indicator. Though different magnitude corrections did accompany some of these patterns, the bull trend remained intact for over a year. The absence of corresponding buy signals (see preceding paragraph) in the oscillators would have resulted in potentially damaging sells, unless losses were limited by stop orders or an exit strategy independent of the oscillator.

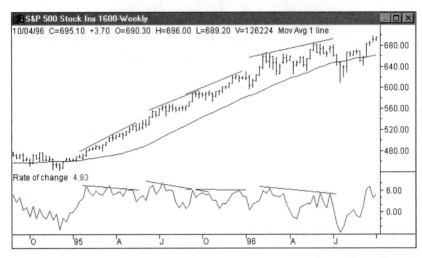

Source: Omega Research

**FIGURE 4.3**   Successive Price Peaks Accompanied by Bearish Divergence Signals in the ROC Indicator

## PERIOD LENGTH REVISITED

The degree of impact of the preceding problems also depends on indicator length. Shorter indicators show less of the effect of a long-term trend. For example, a 5-day stochastic will show less (but still some) of the effect of a long-term trend and will generate more countertrend signals than a 20-day stochastic—at the expense of increased choppiness and false signals. Figure 4.4 illustrates this in the wheat market. The 20-day stochastic spends most of September and October in the overbought zone as a bull trend dominates the market; the 5-day stochastic dips closer to (or into) the oversold zone during the same period.

The 5-day ROC in Figure 4.5 does not include some of the divergences shown by the 40-day ROC but exposes some others; the degree of divergence is also different. The longer the period length of the momentum study, the longer the trend or price cycle it reflects. As a result, equilibrium crossings, extreme values, and divergences occurring in a long-period os-

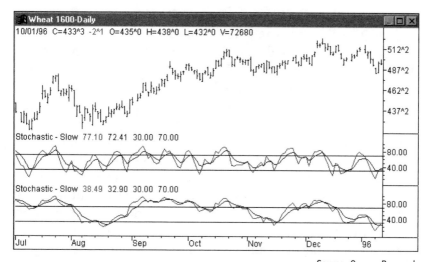

Source: Omega Research

**FIGURE 4.4**   Comparison of 5- and 20-Day Stochastics

cillator are considered more significant than those occurring in a short-period oscillator. If, for example, a 20-day oscillator registers an oversold signal, the subsequent price rally, if it occurs, is expected to be larger than what would occur under the same conditions for a 10-day oscillator—although this is

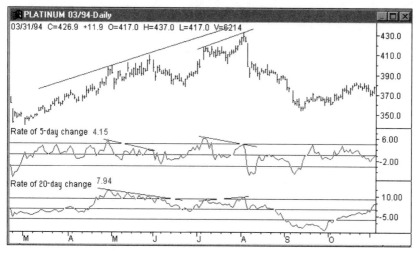

Source: Omega Research

**FIGURE 4.5**   Comparison of 5- and 20-Day ROCs

not always the case. If extreme readings occur in both time periods, the signal is considered that much stronger.

In turn, the period length's impact on the amplitude of the oscillator necessarily influences the level of overbought/ oversold lines. Extreme levels for one period length will be inappropriate for another. Figure 4.6 shows two different-length RSI studies with their extreme zones adjusted accordingly. The 5-day study has zones set at 80 and 20 that capture most of the important swings. The 14-day study has zones of 68 and 32 that still miss some of the peaks and troughs. There is no formula for setting extreme zones at this or that level for a specific period length. The individual indicator and market will dictate placement. The object is to exclude the majority of momentum peaks or troughs to isolate those with the greatest likelihood of signaling a meaningful reversal (depending, of course, on the time frame and how many signals the trader wants to generate). Extreme levels, as noted, do not necessarily have to be symmetrical, that is, equidistant from the equilibrium line; in practice, this would rarely be practical for long time periods because of the effect of changing price direction and market phases.

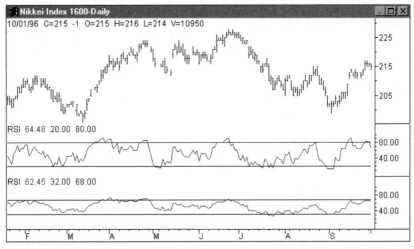

Source: Omega Research

**FIGURE 4.6**   Five- and 14-Day RSI Studies with Adjusted Extreme Zones

## COMBINING OSCILLATORS
## WITH TREND INDICATORS

Oscillator overbought and oversold signals perform much better in trading ranges than in strong trends. Unfortunately, it's
impossible to predict when markets will shift from trending to
trading phases. It is possible, however, to identify the current
market mode (within certain limitations). Figure 4.7 shows
daily cotton with a moving average system using 13- and 34-
day moving averages, a 20-day average directional movement
index (ADX) indicator, and a 10-day slow stochastic, representing a trend direction indicator and trend following system, a trend strength indicator, and a momentum oscillator,
respectively. Using the moving average crossover as a simple trend-following system (buying when the 13-day average
crosses above the 34-day average and selling on the reverse
condition), the other two indicators could be used to time
trade reentries or to generate overbought/oversold trade signals when the market is in a trendless phase that would normally produce whipsaw losses in the moving average system.

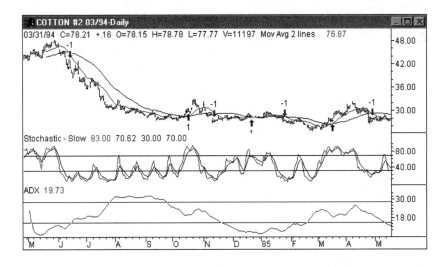

Source: Omega Research

**FIGURE 4.7**  Daily Cotton with a 13- to 34-Day Moving Average Crossover,
Slow Stochastic, and ADX

The period lengths for the different indicators for this example are not optimized and are merely representative: The 13- and 34-day periods for the moving average crossover are popular *Fibonacci numbers* (for reference, these parameters were moderately profitable tested over the 10-year period from 4/2/84 to 3/31/94 using no stops and deducting $100 commissions and slippage per trade); the 20-day ADX gives an indication of the trend strength; the 10-day stochastic is a relatively short- to medium-term momentum study with standard extreme levels of 70 and 30 (an even shorter period, say, 3 or 5 days, would probably be more helpful for purposes like trend reentry). A 10-day RSI serves the same purpose and is used as well in some of the following examples.

Two simple examples suggest the potential interaction of these tools. Like all trend-following systems, this moving average technique is plagued by whipsaws in nontrending periods (note the October through April period in Figure 4.7). A popular goal for trend traders is to reduce whipsaw losses during such periods by standing aside or using an alternate trading method. A simple approach would be to monitor a trend strength indicator like the ADX and stand aside when the ADX suggests the market is not strongly trending. Another approach would be to apply a countertrend technique to sell short-term highs and buy short-term lows—using overbought/oversold signals from a momentum oscillator, for example.

The ADX shows trend strength, regardless of direction (for a further discussion of this indicator, refer to Wilder's *New Concepts in Technical Trading Systems*—see the bibliography). Shorter or longer ADX studies will reflect shorter- or longer-term trend activity. A strong trend—up or down—will be accompanied by higher ADX values. However, it's important to consider the direction of the ADX as well as its level. As a trend reaches its conclusion, the ADX line often levels out. If the market subsequently enters a trading range, the ADX will slope downward gradually (signaling a decreased trend presence, not necessarily a downtrend), and may, for a significant amount of time, still register a relatively high reading. However, it is the ADX's decline, in this context, that indicates the lack of trend. Conversely, ADX readings are frequently at their lowest immediately before the start of a new trend. A significant upturn in the indicator after it has reached a relatively low level (in this example, below 15 was a good approximation) often immediately precedes trending moves. But simply because the ADX is above or below a particular numerical level does not mean the market is or isn't trending. In August and September, for example, the ADX remained at a relatively high level although the downtrend had effectively bottomed out.

Another consideration is that a longer-term ADX study (Wilder's standard value was 14 days), while outlining the general trend strength, will react slowly to quick and dramatic market turns, providing late notice of a shift from trendless to trending market conditions. If, after an extended nontrending period during which a trader would have bypassed the system's trend-following signals, the market embarks on a trend, the ADX may take a while to respond; subsequent potentially profitable trend-following signals may be ignored as a result. The ADX also will sometimes indicate strong directional moves for short-term swings. An additionally smoothed version of the ADX called the average directional index ratio (ADXR) can be used to remove some of the shorter-term noise.

Virtually all the whipsaw periods over 10 years of daily cotton data from 4/2/84 to 3/31/94 coincided with a declining ADX reading below 28 (although some mild trending periods also occurred in these conditions). Trading ranges following strong or lengthy trends were frequently announced by an ADX move below 28. A significant upturn in the ADX after it had moved below 15 coincided with many of the trend phases. Using these general boundaries, it's possible to look for oscillator signals during declining/low ADX periods.

For example, the trendless period from mid-November 1985 to the beginning of May 1986 in Figure 4.8 was marked by a declining/low ADX value and included several moving average whipsaws. As an alternative to standing aside, a trader

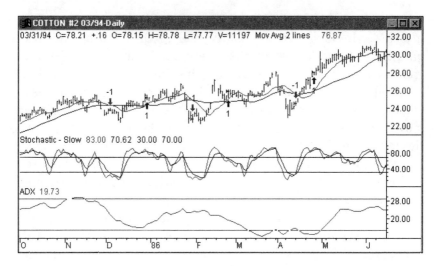

**FIGURE 4.8**   Trendless Period from mid-November 1985 to Beginning of May 1986

could apply a countertrend oscillator technique to buy and sell overbought and oversold extremes. For this time period, both the 10-day RSI and the 10-day stochastic with extreme levels set at 70 and 30 (standard, symmetrical values) generated comparable profits (using no stops and subtracting $100 slippage and commission per trade), whereas the moving average signals lost money (the arrows mark the moving average signals, not the oscillator signals). For example, buying when the 10-day RSI first penetrated the oversold boundary and selling on the reverse condition (taking only the initial signal in either direction) generated in excess of $6,200 in profits while the 13–34 moving average crossover posted a loss of more than $2,600. The oscillator signals are shown in Figure 4.9. This represents, of course, an ideal situation.

In trending periods (denoted by ADX signals that are rising, high, or both), there are still situations in which oscillator countertrend techniques may be useful. If, for example, the moving average system incorporates a profit-taking rule or trailing stop that exits a trend-following position prematurely

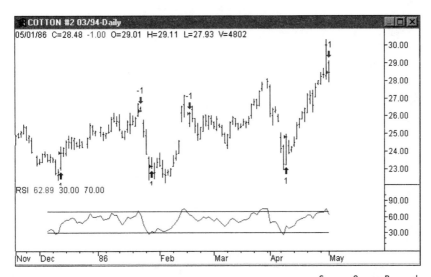

Source: Omega Research

**FIGURE 4.9**   Oscillator Signals during Nontrending Market Phase

(i.e., while the primary system signal indicates the current trend is still in force), oscillator signals provide opportunities to reenter in the direction of the trend. In this case, either the overbought or oversold level requires adjustment to compensate for the trend influence; the oscillator length should be very short (perhaps five days or less) to provide timely reentry. The idea is to buy on dips in an uptrend (signaled by mild oversold oscillator readings) and sell on peaks in a downtrend (signaled by mild overbought oscillator readings). For example, during the downtrend from April to September 1985 shown in Figure 4.10, peaks in the three-day RSI offered several trend reentry points. In this case, an "overbought" level of 60 (established with hindsight) captured most of the opportunities, although a formal level might not even be necessary in some cases: Trend reentries can be executed when the oscillator makes a countertrend peak or trough (regardless of level) and reverses back in the direction of the trend.

The preceding examples outline general applications of oscillator and trend concepts. Though these principles are

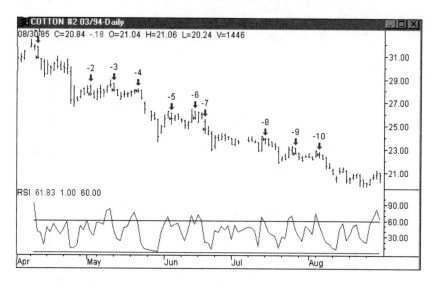

**FIGURE 4.10**    Trend Entry Signals Using Adjusted Short-Term RSI

sound in theory, applying them can be tricky because of the ambiguity of ADX signals, the need to adjust oscillator period lengths and extreme zones to shifting market conditions, and the response time of the indicators as they adjust from trading to trending modes. Avoiding oscillator techniques in disadvantageous market situations is the primary goal.

# 5

## OSCILLATOR APPLICATIONS AND SIGNAL PERFORMANCE

All the factors outlined earlier in Chapter 4—the influence of trend, the inability to know when the market will switch from trending to trading mode, and the shifts in practical extreme zones because of these effects—add to the challenge of *systematically* trading classic oscillator signals using standard, fixed parameters. Over longer time periods, markets will shift from trending phases to choppy trading ranges to stagnant congestion periods. No single indicator or system—oscillator, moving average, astrology, tea leaves—will be effective when traded strictly mechanically in *all* market conditions.

Not surprisingly, most tests of simple oscillator signals as stop-and-reverse systems—buying when the market is oversold, selling when the market is overbought, entering on bullish or bearish divergences, or on signal line crossovers of indicators like stochastics and the MACD—show fairly poor results across many markets and longer test periods. This may, more than anything, indicates that countertrend, systematic applications that do not account for the limitations outlined previously are not the most advantageous ways to use these indicators. For example, in a prolonged uptrend a momentum oscillator may register multiple (or sustained) overbought readings while registering few, if any, oversold readings. A sell trade triggered by one of the overbought signals would never be offset by a corresponding buy signal, and the long position or positions would continue to lose money.

## SIMPLE TESTS

Conducting a few basic tests of the indicators in Chapter 3 on historical data highlights some of the performance characteristics of momentum oscillators. Analyzing the trading rules commonly associated with these indicators provides some of the best insights into the behavior of these tools and how they can be applied more realistically.

One procedure was to test overbought/oversold signals over a range of indicator lengths and extreme levels. The trade methodology was rudimentary: Buy when the indicator became oversold, sell when the indicator became overbought. Only the initial signals in a given direction were acted upon. If, for example, an oscillator pushed into the overbought zone (triggering a sell), subsequently retraced into the neutral zone, and then reentered the overbought zone—before an off-setting buy signal was generated—an additional short trade was *not* entered. All subsequent sell signals were ignored; the next signal that was acted upon was the next buy order, triggered by an oversold reading. Acting on all consecutive signals and liquidating them on the next countersignal (for example, accumulating four long positions and liquidating them at the first available sell signal) produced higher profits in some tests, but at the expense of increasing the drawdown more than tenfold in many cases—beyond any reasonable risk/reward measure. Two specific triggers were tested: upon immediate penetration of the extreme zone and upon retracement of the extreme zone. No stops were used, and $100 dollars was deducted per trade for commissions and slippage. Trades were executed on the close. Nine futures markets were tested, using 10 years of daily continuous data from April 2, 1984, to March 31, 1994: corn, crude oil, cotton, Eurodollars, gold, Japanese yen, live cattle, the S&P 500 stock index, and 30-year T-bonds. This portfolio, though small, represents a variety of market sectors as well as some of the most liquid (and most popular speculative) futures markets in the world.

For comparison, two stop-and-reverse trend-following systems were tested over the same data with the same deduction for commissions and slippage. The first was a channel breakout system: Buys were triggered when price rose above the $n$-day high, sells when price fell below the $n$-day low. The second system used a simple moving average penetration: Buys were triggered when price rose above the $n$-day moving average, sells when price crossed below the $n$-day moving average. Both systems were tested over period lengths from 10 to 100 days, in increments of 5 days.

In the first test, overbought/oversold stochastic signals (regardless of %K/%D crossovers) were tested over a range of period lengths from 4 to 64 days (in increments of 2 days) and equidistant extreme zones ranging from 5 to 45 and 55 to 95 (in increments of 5, e.g., 5–95, 10–90, 15–85, etc.). The tests showed generally negative results and little consistency from market to market or parameter set to parameter set. All the markets except one (the S&P 500 index) posted negative *average* returns over the entire parameter range. Although the high number of days included in the period length range (4 to 20 days would be more representative for countertrend trading purposes) seems to exceed practical trading limits (possibly dragging down the performance averages), the longest period lengths (e.g., 50 or more days) frequently produced the best results in some markets and were sometimes the *only* profitable parameters. These period lengths did, however, result in abnormally long trades with large risk. A test of a smaller 4- to 24-period-length range—more in keeping with commonly used indicator lengths—produced comparable results to the larger test.

Table 5.1 summarizes the average performance of the stochastic signals for each market plus the trend-following system averages. Results are split between the two oscillator entry techniques: The initial penetration method was more profitable than the retracement method in five of the nine markets and was also more successful with relatively shorter period lengths, suggesting that typical short-term countertrend moves might be captured more efficiently by quick action—waiting for the indicator to retrace may give too much back on a trade. However, Table 5.1 shows that the nine-market average figure for the retracement method actually fared slightly better than the average for the initial penetration method. If the extremely positive S&P figures (which buoyed the initial penetration method average) are removed, the retracement method's edge increases substantially.

Three markets—corn, gold, and live cattle—had average figures that outperformed *one* of the trend-following bench-

**TABLE 5.1**  Average Performance of Stochastic Signals plus Trend-Following System Averages

| Market | Channel breakout | Moving average | OB/OS average | OB/OS average | OB/OS average |
|---|---|---|---|---|---|
|  | benchmark average | benchmark average | initial penetration | retracement | Fade signals |
| Corn | ($4,601) | ($15,994) | ($13,085) | ($14,441) | ($8,056) |
| Crude oil | $30,569 | $12,921 | ($39,860) | ($25,356) | $21,369 |
| Cotton | $15,450 | $8,510 | ($29,373) | ($36,333) | $9,758 |
| Eurodollars | $18,521 | $20,221 | ($37,200) | ($14,757) | $20,500 |
| Gold | ($6,575) | ($26,279) | ($6,978) | ($10,210) | ($12,506) |
| Japanese yen | $53,236 | $42,788 | ($68,145) | ($56,611) | $48,439 |
| Live cattle | ($212) | ($16,288) | ($9,959) | ($10,096) | ($11,893) |
| S&P 500 | ($16,505) | ($97,553) | $59,666 | $15,870 | ($82,161) |
| T-bonds | $21,308 | $27,308 | ($49,274) | ($36,777) | $29,315 |
| Averages | $12,355 | ($4,930) | ($21,579) | ($20,968) | $1,641 |

marks, but only the S&P 500 outperformed both. However, the best-performing trend-following average for each commodity outperformed all the standard oscillator averages for the other eight markets. For comparison, the same overbought/oversold tests conducted on the RSI and ROC indicators produced results comparable to the stochastic figures.

The retracement method filters out some false signals (such as would occur if the oscillator remained in an extreme zone for a prolonged period) at the expense of giving back some profit when the market already reverses before the trade is triggered. As a result, it may be worthwhile to consider entering trades (especially when using longer period lengths) on a retracement of an extreme zone, or some defined retracement amount by the oscillator. Exits might be better executed on the initial penetration of a zone. Entries taken *against* the oscillator, that is, buying on overbought signals and selling on oversold signals (see next section), also might benefit from execution on penetration, especially using shorter-term indicators—for example, less than 10 days.

One important note is the relationship between the percentage of profitable trades and the overall profitability of many of these signals. Many parameter combinations had more successful trades than unsuccessful ones. However, the gains on the winning trades were very small compared to the large losses of the losing trades, suggesting that although extreme zones can identify countertrend turning points, the majority of these are corrections in larger trends. A few large losses in these situations outweigh the many gains. Although markets tend to wander more than they trend, the strength of trending periods should not be underestimated.

By comparison, using the trade methodology employed in the original oscillator tests but reversing the direction of the trade—buying when the market was overbought and selling when the market was oversold—actually produced much better results than the traditional trade method. In some of the markets, this approach actually performed on par with, or slightly better than, the trend-following benchmarks. This is tantamount to using oscillators as breakout tools. In Chapter 1 it was discussed how markets often exhibit strong momentum at the beginning of a trend. A decisive move into an extreme zone will accompany a price breakout and is often followed by a sustained trend—hence the success of this method. This phenomenon has been noted in other tests and in fact is the basis of a trade approach called the *stochastic pop,* developed by Jake Bernstein.

Other tests of common oscillator applications generally produced results on par with the initial overbought/oversold tests. For the stochastic, crossovers of the %K and %D lines— buying when %K crossed above %D and selling on the opposite condition—fared worse than the first trade method. Most markets showed no profitable period lengths. However, this lends credence to the standard practice of acting upon crossover signals only when they occur in one of the extreme zones (to filter out whipsaw trades).

Another experiment similar to the first test traded RSI overbought and oversold levels with one difference: The extreme levels, though still sampled in increments of five, were allowed to vary rather than being kept equidistant (90–40, 70–15, etc., not strictly 70–30, 80–20). These optimizations yielded many more profitable (although not necessarily *highly* profitable) parameter combinations and support the idea that static, symmetrical extreme zones are insufficient for varied market conditions over long time periods.

The MACD was tested over the following combinations: the shorter moving average in a range from 10 to 20 days, in 2-day increments; the longer moving average from 22 to 36 days, in 2-day increments; and the signal line from 6 to 14 days in 1-day increments. (Some traders may consider the standard MACD buy-side and sell-side moving average lengths specific rules; for experimentation's sake, we sampled other parameters to see any differences.) Some may feel this violates the MACD approach. However, in no market did the default sell-side parameters of 12–26–9 produce the best results. Trades for the MACD were triggered by signal line crossovers: Buy when the MACD crosses above its signal line and sell when it crosses below it.

Results for the MACD tests underscore the trend-following nature of this basic trade approach. It performed well in trending situations and got whipsawed in congested or ranging markets. Results generally were more favorable in markets with stronger trend characteristics. Table 5.2 shows the optimized MACD parameters for each market over the entire 10-year test period. Overall, performance for this trade signal was slightly better than the overbought/oversold signals outlined previously, which basically underscores the contrast between unoptimized countertrend and trend-following approaches. The optimizations suggest that somewhat longer period lengths (longer than the standard 12–26–9 day) may be helpful. Slightly longer signal lines, especially, can help reduce whipsaw trades. To filter other unwanted signals and to incorporate the countertrend elements of the MACD, crossover trades can be limited to those that occur above or below trader-defined extreme zones, when divergence appears, or in both situations.

**TABLE 5.2** Optimized MACD Parameters for Each Market over 10-Year Test

MACD optimizations: 4/2/84 to 3/31/94 (daily data)

| Market | Short MA | Long MA | Signal | Total profit |
|--------|----------|---------|--------|--------------|
| T-bonds | 16 | 36 | 14 | $3,319 |
| S&P | 12 | 24 | 13 | ($45,525) |
| Yen | 20 | 26 | 14 | $65,737 |
| Crude | 18 | 36 | 11 | $44,170 |
| Gold | 12 | 24 | 11 | $17,450 |
| Cattle | 20 | 36 | 9 | ($18,404) |
| Euros | 18 | 30 | 14 | $2,200 |
| Cotton | 20 | 32 | 14 | ($7,550) |
| Corn | 14 | 22 | 10 | $1,488 |
| Averages | 17 | 30 | 12 | $6,987 |

Another set of tests measured the performance of equilibrium line crossings (as opposed to the standard overbought/oversold technique). Testing period lengths from 4 to 64 days in increments of 2 days for the ROC and RSI indicators yielded profitable results mostly for the longer period lengths. Table 5.3 summarizes the optimized values for the two indicators. As trend-following signals, the equilibrium line crossings were somewhat less successful than the benchmark approaches shown in Table 5.1: The optimized oscillator signals were not always significantly better than the more profitable of the average benchmark figures. Some markets, however, performed very well.

These simple tests are intended simply to give a rough idea of the behavior of some isolated oscillator signals and to highlight the nature of these tools. They should not be considered evidence that these indicators have no value; rather, the tests underscore some of the limitations of their typical applications and the challenges of using them systematically over long time periods in changing market conditions. Adjustments to extreme zones and period lengths and the use of stop-loss orders or independent exit rules (or the decision not

**TABLE 5.3**   Optimized Values for RSI and ROC

RSI and ROC equilibrium line crossings: 4/2/84 to 3/31/94

| Market | RSI length | Total profit | ROC length | Total profit |
|---|---|---|---|---|
| T-bonds | 10 | $31,813 | 38 | $35,144 |
| S&P 500 | 64 | $13,775) | 32 | ($21,675) |
| Yen | 54 | $60,916 | 60 | $82,067 |
| Crude | 30 | $28,860 | 34 | $52,720 |
| Gold | 22 | $23,840) | 12 | ($8,050) |
| Cattle | 58 | ($1,152) | 46 | $11,700 |
| Eurodollars | 20 | $27,125 | 30 | $24,050 |
| Cotton | 52 | $31,660 | 38 | $32,105 |
| Corn | 58 | ($5,362) | 36 | ($3,363) |
| Averages | 41 | $15,138 | 36 | $22,744 |

to use oscillators at all in a given situation) may alleviate some of the problems. But the challenge is knowing when to take such actions.

Similar tests conducted over the years produced comparable results. LeBeau and Lucas, in their book *Computer Analysis of the Futures Markets* (1992, Business One–Irwin), tested several common indicator signals as entry triggers in five markets (soybeans, deutsche marks, gold, T-bonds, and crude oil) over five years of data from January 1986 through December 1990. The percentage of profitable positions was measured at automatic exits 5, 10, 15, and 20 days after entry. No stops were used and no slippage or commissions were subtracted. The oscillator triggers they tested included the stochastic %K/%D crossover (occurring in the overbought/oversold zones only), the stochastic "pop" (which performed slightly better than its standard counterpart), RSI, commodity channel index (CCI; see Chapter 9), and momentum. None tested significantly better than random trade entries—but this was essentially true of all the entry triggers tested, not just oscillators. A second test that used RSI overbought/oversold levels and stochastic crossovers as exit techniques for a benchmark moving average system degraded performance (the stochastic method especially).[1]

Colby and Meyers tested a wide range of indicators and compared them to the performance of a benchmark 40-period simple moving average (SMA) on weekly New York Stock Exchange Index data. They compiled their results in *The Encyclopedia of Technical Market Indicators* (Dow Jones–Irwin, 1988). Of all RSI signals, equilibrium line (50) crossovers tested best; a 21-week RSI had a better return (and risk-adjusted return) than the SMA benchmark. Overbought/oversold indications and divergences produced less-desirable results. For the stochastic oscillator, various combinations of %K/%D crossovers and divergences also posted poor results. Like the RSI, Colby and Meyers found equilibrium line crossings the most profitable approach for the stochastic indicator. The best-case scenario: %K crossovers of the 50 line in a range from 38 to 66 weeks, with 39 the optimal length. For the ROC indicator, longer period lengths (28–38 weeks, 31 weeks best) tested better for equilibrium line crossovers than short periods. The optimal 31-week ROC had a larger maximum drawdown (48.9%), however, than the 40-week simple moving average (SMA) benchmark.[2]

In historical testing, profitable parameter combinations can be found for virtually any indicator, especially when limiting the number of tested markets or the length of the data sample. The value of such optimized parameters on future price action is limited (other than perhaps to find a general range of practical parameters). One specific parameter set—out of, say, a total of 25—that proves to be highly profitable when the rest aren't is merely an example of the computer fitting the rules of the trading system to the available data in great detail. This optimization is unlikely to be profitable in real trading in the future because of the low odds of replicating the precise conditions that resulted in the initial success. The high number of unsuccessful parameter combinations in the oscillator tests puts the smaller number of profitable parameter sets in perspective.

## OSCILLATOR SIGNALS AS WARNINGS

Because of the performance characteristics noted previously, oscillator signals are commonly used as trading alerts: They warn of impending price reversals but should not be used as triggers themselves because of the risk of false signals; instead, trades should be entered only after confirmation by price action (specific price patterns or trend reversals, etc.). Because of the risk of false signals, most traders attempt to incorporate oscillator signals into larger trading plans, using stop-loss and exit techniques to manage the risk of these positions.

Figure 5.1 illustrates several price-reversal indications that can be used after an oscillator registers an extreme read-

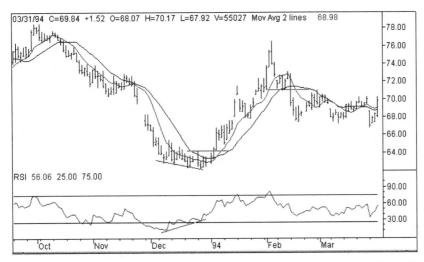

03/31/94 C=69.84 +1.52 O=68.07 H=70.17 L=67.92 V=55027 Mov Avg 2 lines 68.98

RSI 56.06 25.00 75.00

Source: Omega Research

**FIGURE 5.1** Price-Reversal Indications

ing or divergence. The price bottom in heating oil in December is accompanied by an oversold reading in the oscillator and a bullish divergence. Entering on the initial penetration of the oversold zone would have resulted in an early trade and a potential loss depending on the allowed risk for the trade. Entering when momentum returned to the neutral zone would have been hampered by the two quick retracements and dips back into oversold territory. A trader seeking to confirm the trade could wait for reversal signals like a moving average crossover (9–18 days in this case) or an $n$-day breakout (the horizontal line marks an upside breakout of the 5-day high). Similar confirming price reversal signals accompany the market top in February. Note that in January, momentum makes a brief overbought reading; waiting for a price confirmation would have avoided a false signal in this case.

An important consideration here is the value of consulting oscillator signals such as the ones in this example when the price reversal signals function completely independently.

Why bother complicating the matter with oscillator signals when you can simply trade the price signals? Certainly, the oscillator would not impact a mechanical moving average or breakout trend-following system—these signals would take place regardless of momentum patterns of any kind. However, discretionary trading situations may be different. In the case of the December price bottom, the presence of an oversold reading and a divergence would make a strong case for an imminent reversal; the trader could take the liberty of using a shorter-term price reversal signal (like the five-day breakout shown here, or an even quicker pattern) for more timely trades, whereas a trend-following system would normally use a much longer period.

An example of confirming price patterns is the Micro-M tops/Micro-W bottoms described by Thomas A. Bierovic, which identify short-term price entry points in the event of a price/oscillator divergence. In essence, these patterns look for price to initially reverse after a divergence, briefly pull back, and then resume the reversal. In the case of a Micro-W bottom (see Figure 5.2), after a divergence, find a day that closes higher than

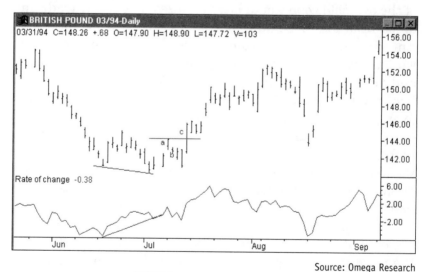

Source: Omega Research

**FIGURE 5.2**   Micro-W Bottom

the previous day's close (price moving in the direction of the expected reversal, point $a$) followed immediately by a day that closes lower (price moving against the new reversal direction, point $b$). Buy on a breakout of the high of the up day/down day sequence (point $c$). Place a stop below the low of the divergence. The pattern is reversed for Micro-M tops.

## SUMMARY

Systematic trading with basic oscillator signals presents many obstacles. Because of the frequency of false signals, extreme readings and divergences usually function as warnings of impending price changes; price reversals are required to enter trades. This, however, calls into question the value of oscillator signals for traders using mechanical, price-based techniques. The next chapter will take a look at some new momentum indicator ideas and innovations to determine what additional insights they can provide about interpreting and trading oscillator signals.

# 6

## INNOVATIONS
## AND MODIFICATIONS

Computer technology has made it easier than ever for traders to experiment with technical indicators and design "new" trading tools. Not surprisingly, momentum oscillators are a popular area of improvisation. But computer testing also has revealed many of the practical trading limitations outlined in preceding chapters. As a result, some of the more recent momentum oscillator innovations attempt to address some of these weaknesses: the skewing effect of trend, the subjectivity of overbought and oversold levels, and the lack of responsiveness of fixed period lengths, to name a few.

This chapter will examine different areas of oscillator construction and interpretation as well as newer indicators and indicator modifications that illustrate particular concepts. These indicators are not the only ones to have emerged in recent years; they simply provide good examples of a number of trading principles and ideas. They are presented not as panaceas to the problems outlined in previous chapters, but rather to give an idea of how traders can experiment to customize momentum indicators to their own needs or create new ones. They also provide additional insight into the role of momentum oscillators in trading.

The basic function and structure of the tools described in this section are essentially the same as those of the indicators we have already discussed. The degree to which they differ—and the practical effect of these differences—varies from case to case. However, the major trading issues—trend versus countertrend, and so on—remain intact. Improvement may be marginal at best. Additional ideas in this chapter relate more to oscillator interpretation than to construction. Unfortunately, some of the more advanced concepts can be covered only in a summary fashion. Readers desiring more information can refer to the bibliography for source materials.

## SMOOTHED VERSUS UNSMOOTHED

When Welles Wilder wrote about the RSI, one of his stated goals was to smooth some of the erratic swings of traditional momentum calculations caused by isolated, extreme price events. To do this, he averaged up and down momentum over the number of days in the indicator: relative strength (RS) = average up closes over $n$ days/average down closes over $n$ days. He also used an additional smoothing technique originally designed to make the day-to-day calculation of the indicator easier (see Chapter 3). Indicator smoothing is not a one-way street, though.

At the most fundamental level, any momentum calculation smoothes price data relative to the length of the indicator: The longer the period length, the greater the smoothing. Additional smoothing has the same advantages and disadvantages it does when present in any other type of indicator—a trade-off between sensitivity and timeliness. A smoothed oscillator, whether an internally smoothed indicator like the slow stochastic or an ROC calculation smoothed after the fact with a moving average, may lack responsiveness to price action. This dampening effect may be valuable in some situations because it removes some of the noise from an indicator, but in others it may obscure important momentum readings. One example of this is the inability of an oscillator to register an overbought or oversold reading. Figure 6.1 compares a 10-day RSI and a 10-day momentum study. Though the indicators are similar, the RSI has much less exaggerated swings. Notice the differences between the two indicators at some of the more significant peaks and troughs, especially the February low after the price peak earlier in the month. The RSI's smoothing causes it to obscure some turning points. Also, the momentum study posted a bearish divergence at the February top while the RSI did not.

As a result, some traders advocate the use of unsmoothed momentum indicators. One example is the Chande momentum oscillator (CMO) presented in the book *The New Technical Trader* (1994, Wiley) by Tushar Chande and Stanley Kroll. The CMO is similar to both standard momentum and the RSI: It is an unsmoothed measurement of price change (like the momentum indicator) and is normalized (like the RSI). It creates an oscillator by dividing the difference between the up and down momentum (directional momentum) by the sum of

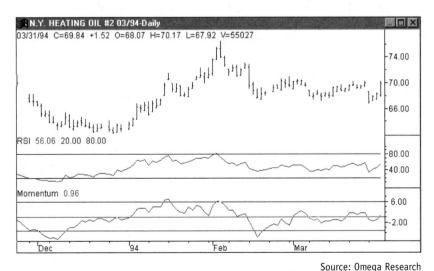

Source: Omega Research

**FIGURE 6.1**  Comparison of Smoothed (10-Day RSI) and Unsmoothed (10-Day Momentum) Oscillators

up and down momentum (nondirectional, or absolute, momentum) over a defined period. The formula is:

$$CMO = 100 * \left[ \frac{(S_u - S_d)}{(S_u + S_d)} \right],$$

where

$S_u$ = sum of the (close-to-close) up-day momentum for $n$ days

$S_d$ = sum of the (close-to-close) down-day momentum for $n$ days

The CMO ranges from 100 to –100 with default overbought and oversold levels of +50 and –50, representing 3:1 and 1:3 up momentum/down momentum ratios, respectively. The CMO differs from the RSI in that (1) it has no internal smoothing calculation, making short-lived momentum extremes more apparent (probably the most important difference); and (2) it includes both up and down momentum in the numerator (the RSI has only up momentum in its numerator). In effect, the CMO is related to the RSI by the following formula: CMO = 2*(unsmoothed RSI) − 100.[1] (The unsmoothed RSI is the formula shown in Chapter 3 without the smoothing process Wilder used to calculate the indicator after the initial period.)

Figure 6.2 shows 10-day CMO and RSI calculations, respectively, and highlights the similarities of the CMO to the RSI (a quick reference will confirm the similarity to simple momentum as well). The CMO does exaggerate some of the more minor price fluctuations and registers more extreme zone penetrations than the RSI, the usefulness of which will depend on the user's need for a more responsive indicator. (Chande and Kroll suggest smoothing the oscillator after calculation if the trader desires.)

Two other examples of unsmoothed momentum oscillators are the TD range expansion index (TD REI) and the TD DeMarker indicator, outlined by Tom DeMark in his book *The New Science of Technical Analysis* (1994, Wiley). Both these

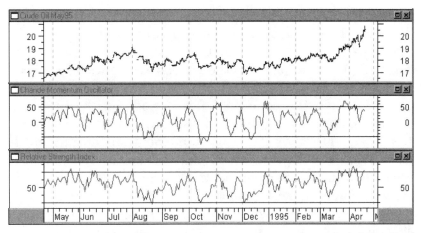

Source: Equis International
**FIGURE 6.2**   Ten-Day CMO and RSI Studies

indicators also use summed (but not averaged or smoothed) momentum. In the case of the TD REI, DeMark's intention was to create an oscillator that would capture market swings but would be unresponsive during both congested periods and extremely steep advances and declines (to prevent buying into a sharp decline or selling into a sharp rally).[2] Two distinctive elements: The indicator calculates momentum of both the high and low prices of the bar (rather than the close) over a two-day period (rather than one-day). The numerator of the TD REI calculation is the difference between today's high and the high two days earlier ($H - H_{t-2}$) plus the difference between today's low and the low two days earlier ($L - L_{t-2}$); these daily figures are summed over a default period of five days. The denominator of the indicator is the sum of the absolute values of the figures in the numerator over the same period ($|H - H_{t-2}| + |L - L_{t-2}|$).

The TD DeMarker indicator, by contrast, divides the 8-day (default length) sum of the 1-day momentum of the highs ($H - H_{t-1}$, 0 if negative) by the high momentum figure from the numerator plus the 8-day sum of the 1-day low momentum ($L - L_{t-1}$, 0 if negative). The TD REI is normalized on a scale from −100 to 100; the TD DeMarker indicator, from 0 to 100. (Because the calculations and exception rules for these indicators are somewhat involved, the steps for creating them are outlined in greater detail in the appendix.) Figure 6.3 shows a 10-day TD REI in the cotton market next to a ten-day RSI. Note the occasional flat periods on the indicator (for example, during the sharp up move in early February 1994). The TD REI's 2-day basic momentum calculation filters out some of the smaller fluctuations apparent in the RSI; because it uses unsmoothed momentum, it also produces more pronounced peaks and troughs.

In general, the use of smoothed or unsmoothed indicators depends on the time frame the trader is operating on and the type of trading he or she is engaged in. Because unsmoothed momentum studies can highlight temporary market extremes, they may be more useful in timing quicker entries and exits. Someone seeking to exit a profitable position may choose a shorter-term, unsmoothed momentum study, whereas someone looking to isolate prominent high and lows might favor a longer-term, smoothed indicator.

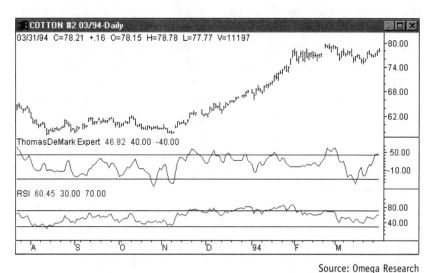

Source: Omega Research

**FIGURE 6.3**    Ten-Day REI and 10-Day RSI

## MARKET CYCLES AND PERIOD LENGTHS:
## INCORPORATING MULTIPLE TIME FRAMES

A common admonition in technical analysis is to consult several indicators to confirm a trading decision. According to this logic, four buy signals are better than one. This first appears to be a benign bit of common sense, but does it really have any practical value beyond providing a psychological safety net? If a confluence of distinct, unrelated trading tools all point to the probability of a particular market event occurring, there may be something to this concept. With most momentum indicators, however, this logic is suspect. The similarity of most oscillators can be seen simply by looking at a chart. The various momentum calculations outlined in earlier chapters also expose the common thread running through different momentum indicators. Correlation analysis provides additional statistical evidence of the close relationship between oscillators. For example, Chande and Kroll's comparison of momentum, RSI, stochastics, the CMO, and other momentum indicators showed very high correlation (all above +.75, where +1 is perfect positive correlation) between indicator pairs applied to identical price data.[3] Because the vast majority of momentum indicators convey virtually the same information, consulting several of them is usually redundant.

However, traders can generally gain greater insight into market behavior by consulting *different time frame* oscillators rather than different oscillators of equal length. Five-day and 40-day ROC studies, for example, will vary much more (and thus give a more complete perspective on market dynamics) than a 5-day ROC and a 5-day RSI. For example, the equal-length ROC and RSI studies in Figure 6.4 look very similar; the short-term and long-term ROC studies in Figure 6.5 are much less alike. Besides the obvious difference of the greater number of times the 5-day ROC study crosses the equilibrium line and posts short-term extremes, it also shows a divergence

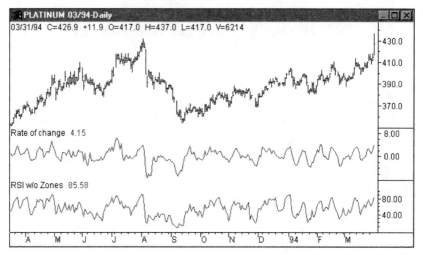

Source: Omega Research

**FIGURE 6.4**   Equal-Length ROC and RSI Studies

between the July and August price highs; the slower study, on the other hand, is much more correlated to the broader market trends and reveals a longer-term, gradual erosion of momentum from April to August that is less apparent on the 5-day ROC.

Source: Omega Research

**FIGURE 6.5**   Short-Term and Long-Term ROC Studies

## PRICE MOVEMENT AS CYCLE INTERACTION

The cyclic model describes the trends, twists, and turns of price action in terms of different time frame cycles at work in the market. An in-depth analysis of the ways to define and identify cycles in the markets can become very technical and is well beyond the scope of this discussion. However, only some major points need to be addressed.

Well-known examples of cycles include the roughly four-year business cycle and the annual seasonal patterns in many agricultural commodities. Other cycles sometimes appear on charts as regular shorter-term peaks or (more commonly) troughs over a given time period (see the pattern of lows and highs in the T-bonds in Figure 6.6). Cyclic analysis describes price patterns as the result of many overlapping cycles operating in the market at the same time—short-term, intermediate, and long-term. Sometimes these cycles are *in phase*—peaking or bottoming at roughly the same time. For example, a strong up move and price top would result from many different cycles all rising and peaking at the same time: The direction and timing of the different cycles reinforce the price

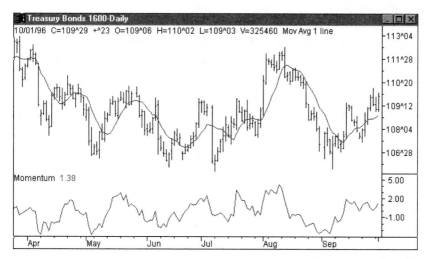

Source: Omega Research

**FIGURE 6.6**   Regular Peaks and Troughs in T-bonds

move. A choppy, more random market (or a congestion period) would result from some cycles peaking while others are bottoming, and so on.

In this sense, different-length momentum studies reflect different-length price cycles—another way of saying that longer-term indicators reflect longer-term price swings, or trends. Consulting different time frame momentum studies can expose the price dynamics of trends or cycles of various lengths. Some momentum studies incorporate different time cycles to reflect this activity in a single indicator.

This idea is not new. Larry Williams, for example, wrote about his "ultimate oscillator" in 1985. It combined 7-, 14-, and 28-day momentum calculations in a single, weighted oscillator (for this indicator's formula and Williams's specific momentum definition, called "buying pressure," refer to Chapter 9). The basic principle can be applied to any momentum indicator: Compute multiple-length momentum calculations that reflect the different time frames you wish to capture (5-day, 20-day, 40-day, etc.). Then sum or average the indicator values to create a composite indicator. Variations include weighting the different components or smoothing them before averaging, depending on the momentum calculations with which you start.

The KST ("know sure thing") is a multiple time frame oscillator approach developed by Martin Pring that integrates four weighted, smoothed ROC studies into a single indicator. It embodies many of the principles outlined earlier.

According to Pring, the strength of a trend is determined by the simultaneous reaction of several cycles. His goal was to construct a tool that, unlike single momentum oscillators with fixed period lengths, incorporated multiple time frames and reflected the different-length cycles, or trends, operating in a market at any given time. For example, important turning points occur when all these cycles are in sync, such as when the short-term, intermediate-term, and long-term cycles are peaking or bottoming. The KST reflects these forces and, by virtue of combining shorter- and longer-term ROCs, enables the longer-term momentum to turn faster while avoiding whipsaws.[4] Some lag, however, is unavoidable in such an indicator.

The KST is constructed by first calculating four different ROCs—for example, 10-period, 15-period, 20-period, and 30-period. These ROCs are then smoothed with moving averages. Next, the smoothed ROC calculations are weighted (from one to four, from the shortest to longest period lengths) and summed. Finally, a 5-period moving average is calculated on the resultant indicator to create a signal line. (While Pring encouraged experimentation with the various ROC and smoothing parameters, he presented default values in his book *Martin Pring on Market Momentum*—see bibliography.) The KST formula can be simplified as follows:

$$\text{KST} = w\text{-period average of } (\text{ROC}_1)$$
$$+ 2*x\text{-period average of } (\text{ROC}_2)$$
$$+ 3*y\text{-period average of } (\text{ROC}_3)$$
$$+ 4*z\text{-period average of } (\text{ROC}_4),$$

where

$w, x, y,$ and $z$ are period lengths for the smoothing calculations (these do not necessarily have to be different—see next paragraph)

$\text{ROC}_1$ is the shortest-term rate-of-change calculation
$\text{ROC}_2$ is a longer-term rate-of-change calculation
$\text{ROC}_3$ is a longer-term rate-of-change calculation
$\text{ROC}_4$ is the longest-term rate-of-change calculation

For example, a short-term KST may consist of the following components: a 10-day ROC smoothed with a 10-day moving average, a 15-day ROC also smoothed with a 10-day moving average, a 20-day ROC smoothed with a 20-day moving average, and a 30-day ROC smoothed with a 15-day moving average. These smoothed ROCs would then be multiplied by one, two, three, and four, respectively, and the results summed to create the final KST indicator. Figure 6.7 displays a KST using the preceding component parameters in the Swiss franc market. The KST follows the broader market turns and filters out short-term

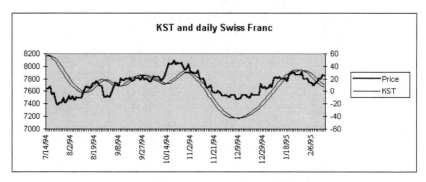

**FIGURE 6.7**   KST in Daily Swiss Franc

noise. There are virtually no signal line whipsaws in this example, but some indicator lag is apparent. Shorter-term traders can adjust parameters to generate more timely signals.

There are three KST signals: (1) when the indicator changes direction, (2) when the indicator crosses its moving average (the best signal, according to Pring), and (3) when the average changes direction. Pring acknowledges the KST may (like other oscillators) give false or premature signals in prolonged uptrends and fail to respond to random events, and because of its smoothing may turn very slowly. Also, KST signals must be confirmed by price reversals.[5]

Long-term (especially smoothed) momentum studies, similar to trend indicators like moving averages, can be used to filter oscillator signals in conjunction with the dominant trend. To this end, Pring designed a KST market cycle model that combines three KSTs constructed with weekly data (and smoothed with exponential rather than simple moving averages) that simulate daily, weekly, and monthly price action. The long-term KST monitors the long-term trend; the intermediate and short-term KSTs are used to time trades. Signals are taken or ignored based on the underlying context of the long-term KST. According to Pring, the best trades occur when the long-term trend (shown by long-term KST) is rising (but not overextended) and the intermediate and short-term KSTs are bottoming (vice versa for bear markets).[6]

## ADAPTIVE TECHNIQUES

Dynamic or adaptive indicators that adjust their parameters
to changing market conditions have become increasingly popular in recent years. Moving averages and channel breakout
systems that change their lengths (usually based on a function of volatility) often show significant improvement over
static indicators that maintain the same number of days in
their calculations. For example, an adaptive moving average
that quickens as the market speeds up and slows down when
prices move sideways in a trading range can track price action more efficiently and reduce whipsaws.

Most momentum studies use fixed period lengths and
fixed reference points like overbought and oversold levels,
making it necessary for the trader to adjust these values as
market conditions change. For example, in a strongly trending market, a trader must adjust the extreme levels to capture useful signals and exclude poor ones. What about the option of using an oscillator that adjusts to trend direction? Or
an oscillator that varies the number of days in its calculation
as volatility increases and decreases? Here are a few techniques that add flexibility to various oscillator elements,
making them more responsive to market dynamics.

The dynamic momentum index (DMI; not to be confused
with Wilder's directional movement index), another indicator
outlined in Chande and Kroll's *The New Technical Trader,*
uses a volatility index to adjust the number of days used in an
oscillator's calculation. The goal is to compensate for the effects of smoothing and the lack of responsiveness to changing
market conditions. This is accomplished by measuring the
current volatility against a benchmark volatility calculation.

The DMI period length increases as volatility drops, and
vice versa: When markets are quiet, the indicator uses a
longer-term perspective. When volatility increases, the period
length tightens, highlighting the short-term price swings.
The author's goal in using a variable-length oscillator was to
overcome the effects of smoothing (that is, obscured short-
lived momentum extremes).[7] The DMI's volatility index (VI)

is the current day's 5-day standard deviation of closing prices divided by the 10-day moving average of the 5-day standard deviation. Using the 14-day RSI as the base oscillator (although a different oscillator could just as easily be substituted), the original period length is divided by the volatility index to generate the new DMI period length. (The authors use upper and lower parameters of 30 and 5 days; these can be adjusted to suit the trader's needs.)

The steps for creating the DMI are as follows:

1. Calculate the 5-day standard deviation of closing prices.
2. Calculate the 10-day moving average of step 1.
3. Pick the initial period length, for example, 14 days.
4. Calculate the volatility index (VI). Volatility index = today's 5-day standard deviation (step 1) divided by today's 10-day moving average of the 5-day standard deviation (step 2).
5. Divide the initial period length (from step 3) by the VI.
6. Define the upper and lower boundaries, for example, 30 and 5 days.[8]

The volatility index in essence provides a measurement of the current relative volatility by comparing today's 5-day standard deviation of prices to the 10-day average of this calculation. (Alternately, a measure like the average true range [ATR] could be used to generate a similar index.) Because the VI increases as volatility increases, the period length shortens with higher VI values. When the volatility index is one (1), the DMI and the RSI will have similar values. When the VI drops below one, the DMI and RSI diverge quickly; when the VI is above one (and increasing), the DMI and RSI diverge slowly.[9]

Signal interpretations for the DMI are standard. Figure 6.8 shows the DMI along with the standard 14-day RSI. Note that the DMI and the RSI are less similar during the trading range period: The VI has dropped and the period length has increased. During the trending period, both indicators tend to

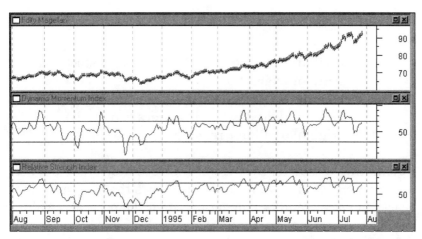

**FIGURE 6.8** DMI with Standard 14-day RSI

remain toward the upper extreme zone, although the DMI's countertrend swings are slightly more pronounced.

A similarly named oscillator that also incorporates an adaptive element—though of a different kind—is the dynamic momentum oscillator (Dynamo) developed by E. Marshall Wall and outlined in the July 1996 issue of *Futures* magazine. The purpose of this technique is to generate a momentum oscillator more resistant to the skewing effect of trend: In a rising market, for example, the indicator posts fewer overbought readings (that might lead to costly sell trades against the uptrend) and more oversold readings (providing more opportunities to enter in the direction of the prevailing trend on corrective dips). Rather than adjusting extreme zones or filtering trades with a trend indicator, the Dynamo modifies the oscillator value itself.

The Dynamo process can be performed on any normalized oscillator (Wall used stochastics in his example). The indicator is adjusted by subtracting the difference between a moving average of the oscillator and the original oscillator reading from the oscillator midpoint. For clarification, the Dynamo formula is:

Dynamo $= M_c - (MA_o - O)$,

where

$M_c$ = oscillator midpoint (50, using the stochastic or RSI, for example);

$MA_o$ = moving average of oscillator (this can be adjusted— Wall used 20-day moving average default); and

$O$ = original oscillator reading.[10]

Calculating a moving average of the oscillator creates a second dynamic equilibrium line that follows the oscillator as it reacts to price trends—moving up when the oscillator values are higher and vice versa. Subtracting the original oscillator value from its moving average discounts the effect of trend; in turn, subtracting this difference from the oscillator midpoint generates a new trend-adjusted oscillator value. When the market is in a trading range, with more regular up and down price swings, the moving average of the oscillator will be close to the normal oscillator equilibrium line, and as a result the Dynamo will be close to the original oscillator reading. During trending periods, the values will diverge. Figure 6.9 shows

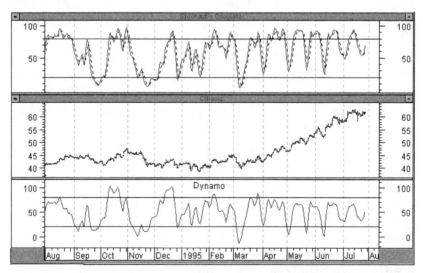

Source: Equis International

**FIGURE 6.9**  Dynamo with 10-day Stochastic

the Dynamo (bottom) compared to the 10-day stochastic (top) from which it was derived. When the market is in a trading range in the latter half of 1994, the Dynamo and the stochastic are very similar. But during the rally beginning in March 1995, the stochastic pushes repeatedly into the overbought zone and fails to post oversold signals. The Dynamo stays below the overbought zone (avoiding false signals) and posts several oversold signals that offered opportunities to enter the market in the direction of the trend. The period lengths for the indicator and the indicator moving average can be adjusted to create a more or less sensitive study.

## DOUBLE SMOOTHING: MOVING AVERAGE LAG VERSUS MOMENTUM LEAD

One of the most notable momentum characteristics is its ability to lead price action (see Chapter 1). Moving averages of price, on the other hand, lag price. What's the result of combining these calculations?

John Ehlers demonstrated with the idealized case of a sine wave that a half-cycle length (e.g., 10 days for a 20-day cycle) moving average lags 90 degrees behind the price series (the sine wave). A momentum calculation of the half-cycle average is in phase with price because of the 90-degree momentum lead[11] (as a result, the half-cycle length is considered the optimum momentum oscillator period length). Figure 6.10 shows an idealized example of the relationships between price, momentum, and moving averages. The T-bond market in Figure 6.6 earlier in the chapter displayed a pattern of fairly regular bottoms (approximately 20 days) in the T-bond market. The 10-day moving average and 10-day momentum calculations on this chart show some of the lag/lead characteristics Ehlers referred to.

In his book *Momentum, Direction, and Divergence* (1995, Wiley), William Blau delved into greater detail regarding the interesting relationships between momentum and moving averages. Blau pointed out that unlike moving averages of

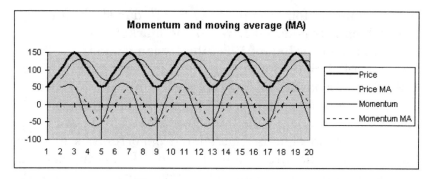

**FIGURE 6.10**   Idealized Price, Moving Average, and Momentum Relationships

price, long-term moving averages of 1-day momentum (e.g., 100, 200, and 300 days) exhibit little or no lag in price determination. In fact, the longer the momentum moving average, the lower the lag.[12] As Blau noted, smoothing prices helps identify the trend and enables traders to position themselves in accordance with it. Directly smoothing prices, however, introduces lag. By contrast, smoothing momentum with a long-term moving average creates a less-noisy price substitute. Applying another level of smoothing (*double-smoothing of momentum*) filters out additional noise and creates a price substitute with little or no lag.[13] Blau pointed out that double-smoothed momentum is an excellent substitute for price *when one of the moving averages is very large.*[14]

Blau constructed several indicators using the double-smoothing concept, which in principle is applicable to momentum calculations of all kinds (he also modified a few existing indicators). One-day momentum (close today − close yesterday) is smoothed with two exponential moving averages (EMAs); as noted, generally only one of the smoothing periods will be very long.[15] The longer average produces the price substitute; the shorter-term average adds another level of smoothing and introduces whatever lag is inherent in the calculation.[16] For example, a momentum calculation smoothed with a 60-day EMA and a 5-day EMA will primarily exhibit lag associated with a 5-day moving average. The formula for Blau's double-smoothed true strength index (TSI) is:

$$TSI = 100 * \frac{[EMA_1\{EMA_2(mtm)\}]}{[EMA_1\{EMA_2(|mtm|)\}]},$$

where
  mtm = 1-day momentum (today's close − yesterday's close);
  |mtm| = absolute value of mtm;
  $EMA_1$ = shorter-term exponential moving average (e.g., 5 days); and
  $EMA_2$ = longer-term exponential moving average (e.g., 60 days).

Note: The order of the smoothing calculations does not matter. In other words, the lengths (short- or long-term) of $EMA_1$ and $EMA_2$ are interchangeable. Alternately, momentum could first be smoothed with a short EMA and the result smoothed with a long EMA.[17] The end result is the same. Period lengths are variable according to the trader's needs.

The TSI creates an oscillator by double-smoothing one-day momentum and dividing it by a double-smoothing of the absolute value of the one-day momentum. Multiplying the result by 100 scales the indicator from −100 to +100, with default overbought/oversold levels of +25 and −25. The TSI, as a result, gives more room for the oscillator to expand after it reaches an extreme zone, unlike oscillators such as the RSI and stochastics that often flatten out and ride the top or bottom of their ranges for extended periods.

The double-smoothed momentum indicator is actually one already encountered in Chapter 2. Both the slow stochastic and the MACD are double-smoothed indicators.[18] The %K line of the slow stochastic is a three-day average (smoothing) of the %D line of the raw fast stochastic; the %D line of the slow stochastic is an additional three-day smoothing of the slow %K. The MACD is the difference between two exponential

moving averages; the MACD histogram is the difference between these EMAs and the exponential signal line—again,
double-smoothed momentum.

Figure 6.11 shows Blau's ergodic oscillator, which is a TSI
with one of the EMA lengths normally set at five and the addition of a five-period signal line (the longer EMA in this case
is 50), together with a stochastic of equivalent length and a
standard 12–26–9 MACD. The ergodic oscillator appears
slightly smoother than the stochastic and somewhat noisier
than the MACD. The TSI/ergodic displays oscillator characteristics like overbought/oversold and divergences, and more
importantly, it functions as a trend indicator (a benefit of its
smoothed composition). The five-period signal line can be
used to generate trade signals in the direction of the trend,
like the MACD. Trend indication can be further enhanced,
according to Blau, by using a 30-period ergodic oscillator
with its fixed EMA set at nine and a nine-period signal line.
This indicator approximates the shape and smoothness of a
12–26–9 MACD, permitting comparison of stocks and commodities on a "normalized amplitude scale." Blau pointed out,
however, that double-smoothed momentum may not accu-

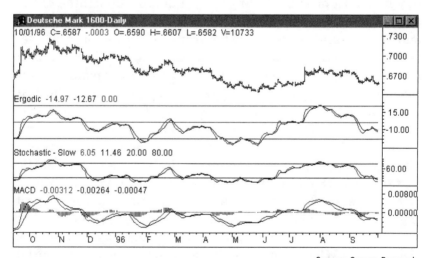

Source: Omega Research

**FIGURE 6.11**   Ergodic Oscillator

rately reflect price direction in congested or trading range markets—directional movement may be implied where none, or very little, is taking place. Directional indications in trending markets are much stronger.[19]

One basic trading technique Blau discussed is to take trades when the slopes of the oscillator and a trend-indicating moving average or long-term TSI are in agreement. For example, in an uptrend, long trades would be executed when both the oscillator and the moving average are rising. When the oscillator and moving average conflict, do not trade. Signal line crossovers trigger entries and exits.

## MAKING USE OF STATISTICS

Although normalized oscillators limit momentum range and allow the trader to establish extreme zones at set distances from the oscillator equilibrium point, these levels are more functions of a particular indicator's construction and period length (and recent market activity) than conclusive definitions of an overbought or oversold market.

One way to make such levels more meaningful is to use statistical measurements to build an oscillator or to establish extreme zones. A simple method that, in effect, creates dynamic overbought and oversold lines is to calculate percentile values of oscillator readings. This concept should be familiar to anyone who has taken a standardized test like the SAT. In addition to the absolute test scores, results are given that show where an individual placed in relation to all other test takers: A score of 90 means a person scored higher than 90 percent of all the other students who took the test. This statistical function, which is available in most spreadsheet programs, can be used in a similar fashion with oscillator values. Calculating a percentile ranking of oscillator values over a given time period (30 days, 40 days, etc.) creates levels that express overbought and oversold as statistical measurements of the data sample. For example, calculating 60-day 90th and 10th percentiles for an oscillator generates overbought and oversold levels, respectively, that identify the upper and lower 10 percent of oscillator values over this time period. Because the days in the calculation move forward as time progresses, these levels adapt to the market. David Stendhal of RINA Systems has developed a similar approach, called Dynamic Zones, using the RSI.

The trader can adjust the number of periods included in the percentile calculation as needed. Long time periods will create a deeper historical context for the extreme levels; shorter time periods will be more relevant to immediate market activity. Figure 6.12 shows a 10-day stochastic with overbought/ oversold levels set at the 95th and 5th percentiles of a

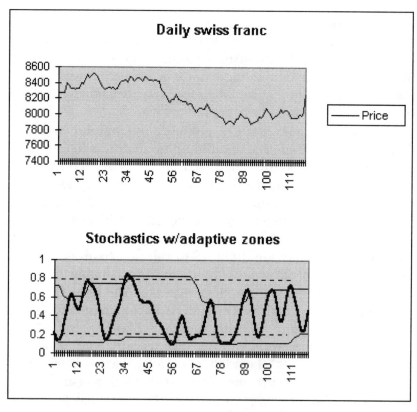

**FIGURE 6.12** Ten-Day Stochastic with Adaptive Overbought/Oversold Levels

moving window of 30 days of oscillator values. (This method can be used on any oscillator, normalized or unbounded.) The horizontal dashed lines represent fixed overbought/oversold levels of 80 and 20. Another idea might be to add adaptivity to this indicator by tying either the number of days used to calculate the oscillator, the overbought and oversold zones, or both to market volatility.

A number of interesting and sophisticated statistical and adaptive techniques are evident in the PeakOscillator, an indicator developed by Cynthia Kase and described in her book *Trading with the Odds* (1996, Irwin Professional Publishing). Kase designed her indicator to replace much of the subjectivity of traditional oscillators with objective calculations, specifically through the use of statistical trend measurements that replace standard empirical measurements (i.e., moving averages).

The statistical formula that was originally at the heart of the PeakOscillator was the random walk index (RWI) described by E. Michael Poulos in the February 1991 issue of *Technical Analysis of Stocks and Commodities* magazine. The concept behind the RWI involves some math that can at first seem somewhat daunting. In short, random systems have certain characteristics that can be identified mathematically. For example, the expected deviation of a random system is equal to the square root of the number of steps, or time units.[20] Poulos used the example of the proverbial drunken sailor staggering in a random fashion. If 100 sailors were limited to taking either 1 step north or 1 step south, after 25 steps the expected average deviation from their starting points would be 5 steps ($\sqrt{25} = 5$).

Transferring this concept into the markets, consider each day a step where the market can go either up or down. The amount it can move can be estimated by the average range over a given period. Accordingly, the expected average deviation of random price change is the average (daily) range multiplied by the square root of time (the number of days, equivalent to the number of steps in the sailor analogy).[21] If the average daily range over a given time period is 10 points, after 25 days, the average deviation of the market would be expected to be 50 points higher or lower ($10*\sqrt{25} = 50$). The RWI divides actual price change by the expected random walk using the following formula. The higher the RWI value—the more price exceeds what would be statistically expected through a random walk—the greater the nonrandom, that is, trending (or, in statistical terms, *serially dependent*) price activity. The formula is:

$$RWI = \frac{\text{actual price move}}{\text{expected random walk}}$$

$$\text{RWI for today's high} = \frac{(H - L_n)}{(\text{avg. range} * \sqrt{n})}$$

$$\text{RWI for today's low} = \frac{(H_n - L)}{(\text{avg. range} * \sqrt{n})}$$

Avg. range is the average range for the preceding $n$ days (Kase used the average true range in her calculations). The period ($n$) that produces the largest index is used as the current day's index.[22] In other words, each day the RWI figures are calculated over a range of lookback periods (say, 5 to 20 days). Whichever lookback period produces the highest RWI—exhibits the greatest degree of nonrandom, or trending activity—becomes the period length for that day. In this way, the calculation adapts to the market, using the dominant cycle at a given time as the indicator length.

It's not difficult to move from this concept to the creation of momentum oscillators. Figure 6.13 shows the 20-day RWI high and low figures (using a 30-day ATR smoothed with a 10-day moving average). Notice the crossover points and how they relate to price direction. Just as subtracting two moving averages (which are empirical trend measurements) creates an oscillator, subtracting the RWI high from the RWI low (statistical trend measurements) also creates a momentum indicator. Figure 6.14 shows the oscillator that results from subtracting the RWI high and low calculations from Figure 6.13. It is im-

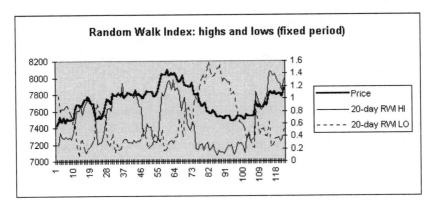

**FIGURE 6.13** Twenty-Day RWI High and Low Figures

portant to note that the examples in Figure 6.13 and 6.14 use a fixed lookback period of 20 days for simplicity's sake. The actual lookback period for a given day would be the one that generated the highest RW value. (Note: In his writings, Poulos suggested the advantage of using two different-length RWIs: Seven to 8 days for a short-term oscillator perspective and more than 8 days as a long-term trend indicator.[23])

Kase's PeakOscillator originally used a *modified* RWI as its foundation. The resultant indicator automatically adapts to the dominant cycle length and also statistically represents

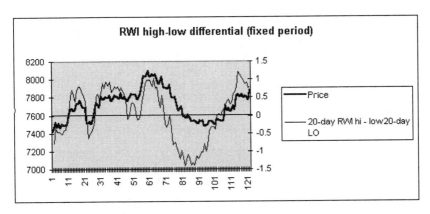

**FIGURE 6.14** RWI High–Low Oscillator

overbought/oversold momentum readings. Because of this statistical basis, the indicator can be evaluated on a distribution curve and the greater of the 90th percentile of historical price data or the 98th percentile of local data used as overbought/oversold zones (Kase tested the indicator over 80 years of data to determine these levels). A penetration and retracement of the resultant "PeakOut" line signals a 90 percent chance of a reversal or a penultimate peak before a divergence.[24]

According to Kase, one of the PeakOscillator's most important benefits is the ability to identify nondivergent turns other oscillators miss.[25] Figure 6.15 shows the PeakOscillator in the crude oil market. The darkened bars mark PeakOut line penetration and retracements; they accompany a few of the more important turning points (note the PeakOut in December 1996 is a penultimate peak before a divergence with the January 1997 high that was followed by a downside correction). Another related indicator, the KaseCD, is the PeakOscillator equivalent of the MACD histogram (which is the difference between the MACD and its signal line): KaseCD = PeakOscillator − average(PeakOscillator,n). An example of this indicator appears in the appendix.

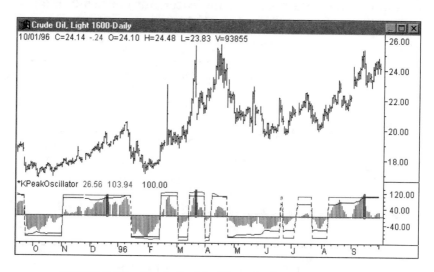

**FIGURE 6.15**     Kase's PeakOscillator in the Crude Oil Market

Kase has since updated the PeakOscillator by replacing the linear measure in the RWI by the same logarithmic approach used in the Black-Scholes model for volatility (see the bibliography for more information on this subject). The application and interpretation of the indicator, however, remain intact.

## THE TIME ELEMENT

Many of the ideas in this chapter revolve around new oscillator calculations or modifications of well-known techniques. Another consideration is the alternative interpretation of signals common to all oscillators.

The most basic oscillator interpretation is the designation of high indicator readings as overbought and low indicator readings as oversold. But because very high or very low readings, as well as prolonged extreme readings, can actually indicate great price strength or weakness (in the case of a strong trend or breakout situation), other factors must be considered to make sense of these signals. Another way to look at overbought/oversold conditions is to consider the amount of time the oscillator spends in an extreme zone.

Tom DeMark, the creator of two unsmoothed oscillators described earlier in this chapter (the TD REI and TD DeMarker; see section on smoothed vs. unsmoothed indicators), also developed rules regarding the relationship of time and the definition of mild versus extreme oscillator values. DeMark believes *mild* overbought/oversold readings correlate better with reversal points than very extreme readings.[26] In his view, historically extreme oscillator readings are evidence of strong momentum in the direction of the signal (such as occurs with breakouts at the beginning of trends) and are a warning to get out of the way of the market. A move by the oscillator back into neutral territory, followed by another less extreme (mild) overbought/oversold signal, identifies a more likely reversal point. The extreme and mild designations, however, are a function of time rather than level: Six days or more qualifies as extreme; less than six days, mild.[27] Such rules provide an additional method to classify oscillator signals rather than strict reliance on numerical high or low definitions.

Figure 6.16 shows the five-day TD REI applied to the T-bill market. In December the indicator registers a strong overbought reading that remains in the extreme zone for seven trading days. A subsequent oscillator peak in January barely touches the overbought level—essentially a one-day reading. This accompanies the final price peak before an eventual downside reversal. Note the relationship between the price and oscillator peaks. Prolonged (six days or more) overbought/oversold readings will often be very high or very low readings because they will occur in a strong trend periods. Overbought/oversold readings of shorter duration often accompany less-forceful price moves (often appearing as a second price high that follows a short sideways period) and will not be as extreme. As a result, this type of time analysis frequently locates the type of classic divergence found in this example.

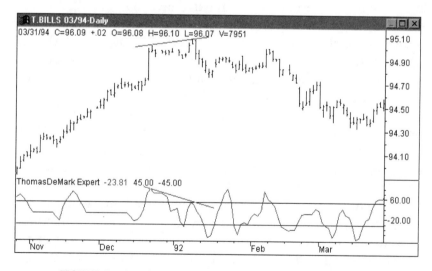

**FIGURE 6.16**   Five-Day TD REI Applied to the T-Bill Market

## SUMMARY

The ideas in this chapter illustrate that no approach or indicator is sacred—experimentation is advisable and even necessary if a trader wants to completely grasp a particular technique. No parameters (period lengths, extreme zones, etc.) or interpretations are carved in stone; they should be considered starting points for individual research and innovation. These new indicators and modifications also show the different techniques that can be used to address the flaws in any indicator. However, it's also very clear that, regardless of the type of innovation, the basic trading issues and applications remain constant. Visual inspection of the examples in this chapter highlight the similarities to traditional oscillators; they are not radically different tools. The risk inherent in countertrend trading techniques can be managed but not removed.

For reference, Chapter 9 includes several other brief oscillator descriptions and formulas not included here.

# 7

## OTHER ISSUES: DIVERGENCE, LONGER TIME FRAMES, AND PRICE INPUTS

Few aspects of momentum oscillators are as widely followed and closely scrutinized as divergence. This also is one of the most challenging aspects of these indicators to interpret. Many of the issues associated with overbought and oversold readings—repeated false signals and distortions related to strong trends and extreme price action—impact divergence analysis as well.

Divergence, as outlined in chapters 1 and 2, refers to an oscillator's failure to confirm a price move—that is, to match a higher-price high with a corresponding new momentum high or a lower-price low with a corresponding new momentum low. These classic divergences are familiar to any trader who has plotted a momentum study at the bottom of a price chart (see Figure 7.1). They imply that momentum is not supporting the market's case: A market may push higher, but if

Source: Omega Research

**FIGURE 7.1** Classic Divergences

momentum fails to do likewise, the move may be vulnerable. Accordingly, traders can prepare for a possible correction or reversal, protecting current positions or establishing new ones in anticipation of a new trend. Divergences are actually quite common, appearing at many market turning points and on various time frames. Many of them are, in fact, followed by significant reversals.

The problem is determining which patterns are more likely to result in such reversals. It's very difficult to make sweeping statements about divergences. Few common denominators link those that precede meaningful reversals, in contrast to false ones that appear repeatedly in strongly trending markets. Trading divergences is an inherently anticipatory approach designed to locate new price moves as early as possible, as opposed to following established trends. As a result, divergences, like overbought/oversold signals, are commonly used as warnings of potential price developments; action is not taken until a definitive price reversal occurs. Because repeated divergences can occur in trending markets, traders are sometimes advised to use divergences only in trading markets. However, because divergence analysis is frequently applied to locating significant, longer-term reversal points rather than shorter-term swing points, it will unavoidably put the trader in the position of operating against the trend. Although divergences do appear on the smallest time frames, it is generally more productive to focus on longer period lengths or long-term charts (weekly, monthly) to monitor larger-scale price action (see next section).

## DIVERGENCE VARIATIONS

The classic divergences shown in Figure 7.1 represent a clear and easily understood relationship between price and a momentum indicator. But not all examples are as simple. Consider the basic divergence issue: A price move is not supported by equivalent momentum. But what about mitigating factors like the degree of divergence? Does a bearish divergence in which the divergent momentum peak is dramatically lower than the preceding peak have more significance than one where the peak is only slightly lower? The basic divergence concept—that price exhibits one kind of behavior while momentum displays another—can manifest itself in various ways.

For example, take a market that makes an extremely strong new high or low while momentum remains flat. Though not a classic divergence, this is certainly a case where momentum does not confirm a price move. Taking this concept one step further, consider the case of a market that again makes a forceful drive to a significantly higher high, while momentum also makes a higher high—but only incrementally (say, one or two points). Although momentum has technically moved in the same *direction* as price, it has done so only marginally—it is not matching the price strength with comparable momentum strength. Consider also the case of price making a double top, where the second top is the same as the first, or only incrementally lower, but the second momentum peak is dramatically lower than the first. Price has essentially remained static while momentum has weakened—again, not a classic divergence, but certainly a clash between the price and momentum messages. Brief study of a few charts reveals that these patterns often accompany price reversals—just like classic divergences.

Another issue is the interpretation of serial divergence patterns. Like overbought and oversold indications, good divergence signals can be overwhelmed by false ones in prolonged trends. It is unlikely that a clear-cut, single divergence will occur only between the second-to-last and last peaks or troughs of a price move. A long price uptrend, for example, contains many lesser peaks before it finally tops and reverses: Several intermediary divergences may occur among these points. Figure 7.2 shows a weekly chart of the S&P 500 index during the strong bull market in 1995. Several divergences are apparent, beginning fairly early in the year.

Multiple divergences are often considered more significant than single or double divergences (indicative of larger reversals).[1] In retrospect this may be apparent, and it does makes sense. The longer the trend (and by definition, the closer it is to conclusion), the more divergences are likely to occur; also, a long-term trend reversal is likely to be more dramatic than a short-term trend reversal. So, multiple diver-

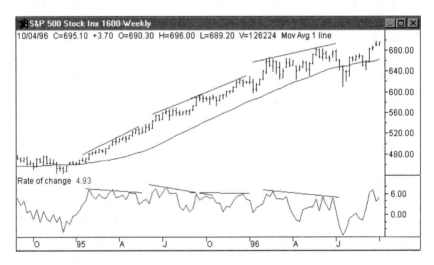

**FIGURE 7.2**   Serial Divergences in a Sustained Bull Move

gences become associated with major turning points. The problem is knowing *which* divergence in a series is the last.

## JUDGING SIGNALS

Despite these complications, divergences *can* accompany excellent reversals. But if the market does not reverse after a divergence in a trending market, a lack of signals in the opposite direction will offer no exit points; losses are uncontrolled unless a stop-loss is in place. For example, testing a simple divergence system that sells on a classic bearish divergence and buys on a classic bullish divergence (using a 14-day RSI), coffee futures proved to be unprofitable from June 1, 1993, through October 1, 1996. Adding an arbitrary $1,750 stop-loss and a $5,500 profit target made the system profitable, reaffirming inherent risks of the basic system—as well as the fact that the divergences identified some tradable reversal points (outnumbered, unfortunately, by the bad signals in this case). However, even these results underperformed an unoptimized 9–18 day moving average crossover system for the same period.

As a result, traders use various filter techniques to isolate those divergences with the greatest odds of success. Most of these rules have to do with the time difference between the price and momentum extremes and the level at which the divergence occurs. For example, one of the most common rules is to ignore divergences unless they take place in either of the extreme zones. The logic behind this is not difficult to understand. Because a move into overbought or oversold territory indicates a higher probability of a price reversal, a divergence in these zones exposes momentum weakness when the market is presumably overextended. (Only the initial momentum extreme need be in the extreme zone; a significantly less severe momentum peak or trough accompanying the divergent price extreme indicates greatly reduced momentum and is commonly interpreted as additional confirmation of the signal.)

Divergences very close together or very far apart are also associated with low success rates. Specific limits are vague, but periods of two to five days on the short end and 10 to 12 weeks on the long end are common. LeBeau and Lucas, for example, found RSI daily divergences closer than "a few days" or farther apart than 10 weeks to be poor signals.[2] Divergence signals are further judged according to the time frame in which the trader is operating; the importance of a divergence is commensurate with the size of the price move of which it is a part. For example, divergence in a shorter-term move suggests the possibility of a small reversal, whereas divergence in a larger-scale trend implies a more significant reversal.[3] Short-term divergences are not really relevant to the intermediate- or longer-term price action.[4] A good rule of thumb, though, is to check if the peaks or troughs in question can reasonably be considered part of the same price pattern. The momentum relationship of two peaks separated by eight months and two distinct trend phases on a daily chart is meaningless.

Finally, price is commonly considered the final trade determinant. Like overbought/oversold signals, divergences should not be acted on alone (according to popular wisdom); they should be confirmed by price action—a series of closes in the direction of the new trend, a trendline break, a chart pattern, and so on.[5] They are considered warnings of potential price developments, not trade signals themselves. Though this is prudent advice, if true, the trader should investigate the merits of trading the price pattern that eventually triggers the trade and see if divergence really impacts results in one way or the other.

One overlooked issue is to make sure that a divergence actually takes place. When locating classic divergences, traders commonly draw a line connecting two or more ascending price peaks or descending price troughs—using the highs and lows of the respective price bars. Care must be taken, especially when the price peaks or troughs in question are fairly close in time (roughly a week or less), fairly close in price, or both. What appears as a higher price measured by the high of the bar might actually be a *lower* high based on the closing price; both the price and momentum peaks are lower, and no divergence (at least no classic divergence) actually takes place.

Because most indicators use the closing price (rather than highs or lows) in their calculations, the position of the close in an important bar at a market turning point can greatly affect a technical indicator's reading. For example, the phenomenon known among chart analysts as a *key reversal day* at a price peak (a higher high with a low close) will commonly coincide with a divergence signal from a momentum oscillator using closing prices. The closer together in time two possibly divergent price peaks or troughs are, the more likely they'll be closer in price, increasing the odds of a "phantom" divergence. Figure 7.3 shows what appears to be a classic bullish divergence on a bar chart as a phantom divergence on a closing price chart (immediately below the bar chart). It should be noted, however, that such patterns are also often followed by reversals, as occurs in this instance.

The opposite situation can also occur. At the end of an uptrend, for example, price may form a double-top, with the high of the second peak slightly lower than that of the first peak. If momentum also makes a lower high on the second peak, it would simply appear to be mimicking the price failure swing. However, the closing price of the second peak may actually be

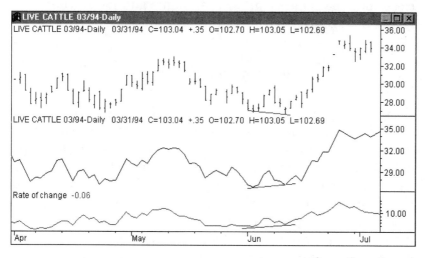

Source: Omega Research

**FIGURE 7.3**   "Phantom" Divergence

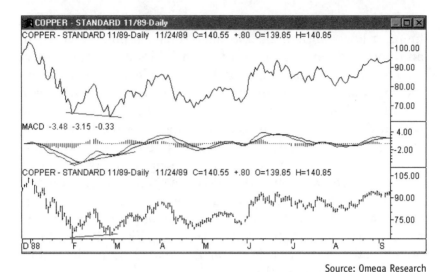

Source: Omega Research

**FIGURE 7.4**   Classical Bullish Divergence Camouflaged by Price Extremes

higher than that of the first peak; as a result, a classical bearish divergence is camouflaged by the extremes of the price
bars. Figure 7.4 provides an example of this phenomenon. At
any rate, using closing price charts reveals the true relationship between price and momentum extremes. Connecting
closes on a bar chart (rather than highs and lows) when analyzing divergences will serve the same purpose.

## DIVERGENCE EXAMPLES

Table 7.1 summarizes the divergence characteristics of a 10-
day RSI at some of the more significant tops and bottoms in
the corn market from April 2, 1984, to March 31, 1994 (a 10-
day ROC, 14-day stochastic, and standard 12–26–9 MACD
were also monitored for comparison). The reversal points
were located on a weekly chart (see Figure 7.5) to give a
longer-term perspective, and then price behavior was ana-
lyzed on a daily chart. Only four of the twelve reversal points
did not post classic divergences (although two bottoms had
essentially flat momentum between their component price

**TABLE 7.1** RSI Divergence Analyses

Daily corn: 4/2/84 to 3/31/94

| Date | Price (close) | Top | Bottom | Classic divergence | # | # trading days | Relationship to extreme levels and other characteristics |
|---|---|---|---|---|---|---|---|
| 9/9/85 | 369.5 | | X | Yes | Single | 24 | First trough in overbought zone; divergent trough in neutral zone. |
| 5/14/86 | 406.75 | X | | Yes | Double | 8 | All peaks in overbought zone. |
| 6/16/87 | 373.25 | X | | Yes | Single | 26 | Both momentum peaks in overbought zone. |
| 8/7/87 | 317.25 | | X | No | | | Momentum flat/slightly lower than previous trough. Note: Equivalent ROC posted multiple divergence pattern. |
| 6/27/88 | 486 | X | | Yes | Single | 2 | Both peaks in overbought zone. |
| 8/3/89 | 328.75 | | X | No | | | Flat/declining momentum. Note: Equivalent ROC posted short-term double divergence. |
| (5/2/90)- 7/3/90 | 389.75 | X | | Yes | Single/ triple | 15/ 39 | Both peaks of the single divergence from 6/12 to 7/3 in neutral zone; this divergence was part of larger divergence pattern beginning 5/2/90, with momentum in overbought zone. |
| 7/12/91 | 300.75 | | X | Yes | Single | 6 | Both troughs in oversold zone. |
| 8/2/91 | 343.5 | X | | No | | | Peak in extreme zone. |
| (1/15/92)- 3/9/92 | 338.75 | X | | Yes | Single/ triple | 21/ 40 | All peaks in overbought zone. Part of a larger divergence pattern back to 1/15/92. |
| 6/16/93 | 241.5 | | X | No | | | Trough in extreme zone. |
| 1/14/94 | 317.5 | X | | Yes | Double/ quadruple | 9/ 36 | First peak in extreme zone; second and third in neutral zone. This was part of an extended pattern beginning on 11/17/93. |

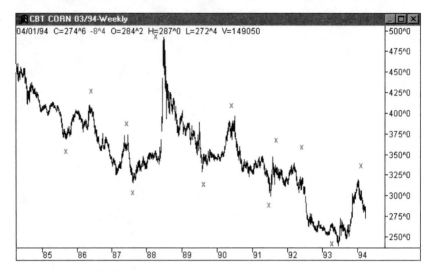

**FIGURE 7.5**    Significant Reversal Points in Weekly Corn

troughs). The patterns showed a great deal of variation in the number of divergences, the number of days separating them, and their locations relative to the extreme zones.

In addition to the signals summarized in Table 7.1, well over 30 distinct divergence patterns occurred during this time period, the majority of which were either false signals during trends or precursors to insignificant corrections or reversals. There was very little difference between the RSI and the ROC studies (the ROC registered a few more divergences, mostly short-term). Stochastics posted slightly fewer divergences, perhaps because of the somewhat longer time period. The MACD gave still fewer signals because of its longer time frame and smoothed composition.

Isolating divergences in the extreme zones was of little benefit for this data sample. Several divergences that occurred in the extreme zones preceded insignificant reactions or were followed by additional divergences. Because of trend strength, the indicator occasionally spent extended periods in an extreme zone; divergences were inevitable during these periods. But because the placement of extreme zones depends on the period length of the indicator and the direction and degree of trend in the market at a given time, these distinctions are unavoidably subjective.

In some cases, the difference in price tops or bottoms (using closing prices) was as little as one tick (although using the highs and lows of the bars made the difference appear much greater). Similarly, momentum peak and trough differences were sometimes very insignificant. However, neither of these factors seemed to have much correlation to either the accuracy of a particular divergence signal or the magnitude of the subsequent reversal. Neither did the time difference between the divergence points. One of the quickest and most dramatic reversals occurred after a two-day divergence. (A study by William Brower of a mechanical divergence system also found that limiting signals to divergences greater than five days degraded system performance.[6]) Also, marginal-divergence patterns (i.e., flat momentum instead of strictly divergent momentum) were often as successful as classical divergences (see Figure 7.6). These patterns suggest it may be advantageous to place more emphasis on the relative *price* level (i.e., historically high or low prices) rather than the

Source: Omega Research

**FIGURE 7.6**  Lower Price Low Accompanied by Flat Momentum

severity of the divergence, and to monitor longer time frames and longer indicators to filter out shorter-term, meaningless signals.

Some of the better signals occurred at slow-developing rounded or double tops. Instances where the market made a strong peak or trough (sometimes containing shorter-term, small-magnitude divergences), subsequently entered a trading range of approximately two weeks or more, and then made a run for new highs or lows (posting divergence with the previous major peak or trough) led to some of the quickest and most forceful reversals. Most of the divergences at the major turning points were single or double divergences (although some of these were part of longer-term complex divergences). LeBeau and Lucas found double and triple divergences more prevalent in trending markets, with single divergences more common in trading markets.[7]

In a strong trend, a divergence should not be expected to automatically result in a substantial reversal; traders should be patient through at least one or two divergences in such a situation, although this will undoubtedly result in missing some turns. Looking for divergences only in extreme zones is probably a good way to better the odds of this technique's success, but in a trending move the oscillator should have entered the zone at least once or twice (to guard against early, false signals) prior to the ultimate divergence pattern. Again, these signals can only be considered warnings; price reversal confirmation is mandatory.

Because classic divergence signals frequently provide such powerful visual images, many traders follow them. However, a closer look at the variety of guises the divergence concept can adopt shows how complicated this trading issue is. The line between what constitutes a divergence and what doesn't becomes blurred. What technically qualifies as a divergence between price and a momentum indicator can be obscured by the extremes of price bars; conversely, something that appears to be a classic divergence on a bar chart may not appear as such when closing prices are compared.

## CONSULTING DIFFERENT TIME FRAMES

As with other aspects of momentum analysis, looking at different-length indicators can provide insight about the dynamics of different price trends or cycles that may impact divergences. Quick divergences separated by only a few days may appear on a short-term but not a long-term oscillator. Longer-term studies can obscure divergences at short-term (and occasionally at long-term) points as well.

Longer-term or smoothed indicators like the MACD (or the TSI from Chapter 5, or even a long-term slow stochastic) may not produce distinct peaks or troughs to compare with the corresponding price extremes and so will sometimes miss shorter-term divergences, especially in accelerated tops or bottoms. As a result, divergence may have to be determined on the basis of the direction of the indicator's slope—does it or does it not coincide with price direction? However, these indicators often give less-ambiguous, more-pronounced divergence signals at slower-developing peaks, as shown in Figure 7.7 (MACD signal

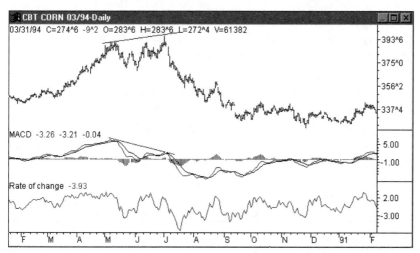

Source: Omega Research

**FIGURE 7.7**   Divergence Signal Highlighted by Longer-Term, Smoothed Indicator

line crossovers also supply clear trade triggers at these points). The ROC shows only a less-pronounced, shorter-term divergence between the June peaks. These characteristics (a product of the stronger trend-following components of these tools) make the MACD and similar indicators well suited to highlighting divergences at many significant turning points.

## WEEKLY AND MONTHLY CHARTS

Applying momentum analysis to weekly and monthly charts gives the trader a longer-term perspective—and frequently a more advantageous setting in which to use oscillator signals. One reason for this is that trending price activity on shorter time frames often reveals itself to be swing movement in a longer-term cyclic market pattern. Because oscillators give better signals in trading ranges rather than trending markets, using a time frame that emphasizes this aspect of the market will benefit oscillator-based approaches. Tops and bottoms located with extreme zones and divergences will more likely isolate major reversal points (because of the larger time/price scale) that can subsequently be exploited with shorter-term trade signals. This characteristic is by no means universal—trend characteristics in some instruments are more apparent on longer time frames—but it is certainly a viable area of research and experimentation.

Figure 7.8 shows 10 years of monthly wheat data and an unoptimized 10-period RSI with overbought and oversold levels set at 70 and 30, respectively. The oscillator captured virtually all of the major tops and bottoms over this period (it missed the 1992 low); the upswing in 1991, coincidentally, also was announced by a classic bullish divergence. Although trading such signals mechanically would be difficult because of the large time/price scale, such an approach may still aid in isolating long-term market turning points. Entry and exit strategies can be executed by moving down to the daily time frame using price-based techniques.

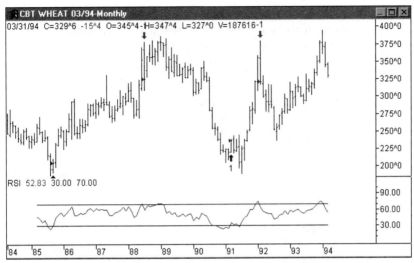

**FIGURE 7.8**  Applying a 10-Period RSI to Monthly Wheat

## EXPERIMENTING WITH PRICE INPUTS

The closing price of a bar chart is by far the most common input of technical indicators. It is a representative price: A close-only chart essentially functions as a simplified or smoothed price series because intraday noise is removed. Also, the close has special prominence because of its behavior at key market junctures. Its relative position may underscore trend strength or signal possible reversals. The tendency of the market to close in the direction of dynamic, short-term price swings and chart patterns like the key reversal day come to mind.

With a handful of exceptions, the indicators in this book are constructed using closing prices. Substituting other price inputs—the high, low, or average price of a bar—can create subtle (and occasionally not-so-subtle) changes in an oscillator's behavior. Is there any advantage to doing this? It's possible to draw some conclusions by examining the differences in an oscillator when various price inputs are used.

Figure 7.9 shows the daily S&P 500 with two 14-day RSIs. The one immediately below the price series uses the average price of each daily bar in the RSI formula; the second is the standard RSI constructed with the closing price. Differences are immediately apparent. The average price used in the modified RSI creates an additional level of smoothing—the indicator is less noisy than the standard RSI; also, the modified RSI has more pronounced countertrend swings (note the oversold signal in April 1997). On the other hand, the modified RSI posts more overbought signals throughout the course of the uptrend.

Figure 7.10 compares an indicator constructed with high prices (RSI-high) to a standard closing-price RSI. The RSI-high indicator tends to push to the upside a little more than its generic counterpart, which is not surprising. However, some of the downside swings are more pronounced as well, especially the April 1997 low that displays a classic bullish divergence not apparent on the standard RSI. Again, the modi-

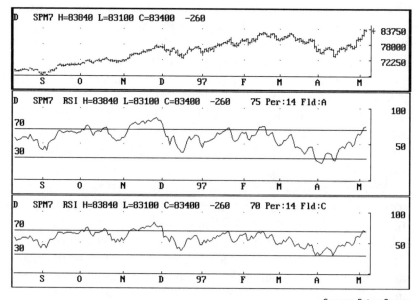

Source: FutureSource

**FIGURE 7.9**   Comparison of RSIs Using Average and Closing Prices

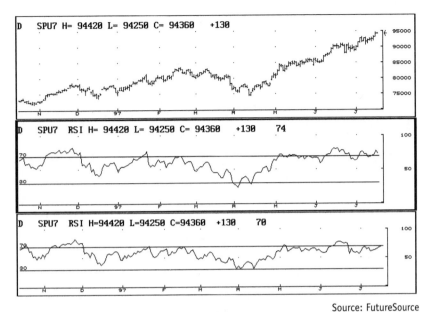

Source: FutureSource

**FIGURE 7.10**   Comparison of RSIs Using High and Closing Prices

fied indicator is slightly less noisy. Figure 7.11 compares RSIs using low prices and closing prices, respectively. Like the RSI-high example, the RSI-low modestly exaggerates both over-bought and oversold readings at many swing points and is slightly smoother than the RSI-close.

A somewhat different picture appears when the same technique is applied to a simple, unsmoothed indicator like momentum. Figure 7.12 shows 20-day momentum calculated with both highs (immediately below the price series) and lows. There is a greater delineation of exaggerated over-bought signals with the momentum-high and exaggerated oversold signals with the momentum-low. (Interestingly, the momentum-high tends to magnify both overbought *and* over-sold extremes to a greater degree than the momentum-low.)

This information can be applied to oscillator construction in a number of ways. Tom DeMark, for example, incorporated the tendency exhibited by the momentum examples in his TD ROC II indicator, which is a rate-of-change calculation that

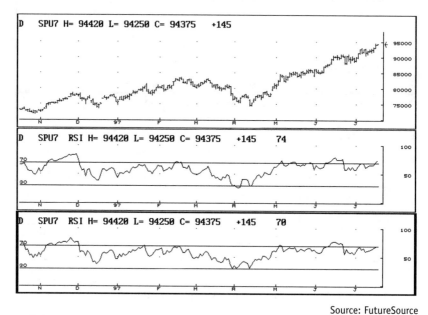

Source: FutureSource

**FIGURE 7.11**   Comparison of RSIs Using Low Prices and Closing Prices

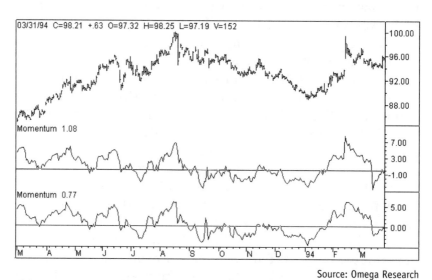

Source: Omega Research

**FIGURE 7.12**   Twenty-Day Momentum Calculated with Both Highs and Lows

uses default overbought and oversold levels of 102.5 and 97.5 (using the ROC formula $100*P_t/P_{t-12}$; 100 is the equilibrium line). The indicator uses high prices in its calculation when the indicator moves above its equilibrium line and low prices when it moves below the equilibrium line. Accordingly, momentum extremes are highlighted. DeMark also noted the threshold that initiates the switch from high to low prices can be changed according to the user's needs (to a point between the equilibrium line and an extreme zone, for example). This technique, of course, is applicable to any oscillator normally constructed with closing prices.

# 8

## CONCLUSION: OSCILLATORS IN CONTEXT

Momentum oscillators convey a great deal of information: potential exhaustion points as well as general trend direction and strength. They can be used to establish new trades in or against the direction of the trend, to liquidate open positions, or to adjust stop levels to protect profits. This flexibility means little, however, if these tools are not appraised realistically. Oscillators have significant practical limitations.

Momentum oscillators (generally) function as detrended smoothings of price: They highlight shorter-term market extremes and filter out trend relative to indicator length. Though the number of momentum-based oscillators seems to grow almost daily, breaking down the various formulas reveals a handful of related ideas that ultimately flow from the basic momentum principles and calculations outlined in chapters 1 and 2. Momentum indicators have an inherent leading characteristic: They highlight trend dissipation through divergence and can give advance warning of market reversals, which can make them extremely useful tools in discretionary analysis and forecasting situations. Although they are often portrayed as such, oscillators are *not* mechanical trading systems that should operate independently of other entry or exit signals or money-management techniques.

Momentum oscillators can effectively isolate market extremes and warn of impending reversals. From this perspective, they are much better suited to nontrending markets than to trending markets; because markets range more than they trend, the use of countertrend oscillator techniques would also seem to be logical. However, trading traditional oscillator signals in a *systematic fashion*—buying when the indicator is oversold, selling when it is overbought—can be risky because the number of false signals caused by the influence of trend and the subjectivity of indicator parameters like period lengths and extreme thresholds. Also, though tools like trend strength indicators may indicate (with a certain amount of lag) what phase the market is currently in, it is impossible to know precisely when a market will *switch* from trending mode to trading range mode and back again, making it difficult to effectively time the most advantageous periods in which to use oscillators. On their own, momentum indicators are dangerous trade guides.

As a result, it's important to view oscillator signals in the context of a particular market situation. An extreme oversold oscillator reading that occurs in the midst of an ongoing bear trend should not necessarily be considered an automatic buy signal. If a longer-term trend indicator suggests the market is still in a downtrend, it is likely the signal is one of many false readings caused by the strong directional bias. Another practical trading consideration that comes into play includes the precise timing of oscillator-triggered trades. When entering trades based on extreme readings, trades could be entered upon initial penetration of the extreme threshold, retracement of the extreme threshold, or an *n*-point reversal of the indicator when it is in the extreme zone. The difference in using one or another of these methods can dramatically impact the success of a given trade because short-term trading opportunities are just that—quick to appear and disappear; their potential profit time horizon is very limited. Traders must choose between acting quickly on a signal and waiting for confirmation that may result in giving back a substantial amount of the profit on a corrective move.

Because of the factors outlined here, oscillator signals are often cast in the role of secondary indicators, or market *alerts:* they warn of potential price developments. Price-based signals like breakouts, moving-average crossovers, chart patterns, and so on, function as the actual trade triggers. This kind of discretionary integration of oscillator signals is likely to be more useful for most traders than independent, systematic applications. However, it also raises the question of the added value of the oscillator in such situations: Because the price-based trade signals would occur regardless of the activity in the oscillator, the trader must determine whether the oscillator signals improve the performance of a trading system by filtering out low-quality trades.

The newer indicators and innovations outlined in Chapter 6 (and in the appendix) represent efforts to address some of the challenges of trading with oscillators: accounting for trend influence, balancing the noise reduction of smoothing with the responsiveness of unsmoothed calculations, establishing objective overbought/oversold zones, using statistics to create indicators that are more objective, creating indicators that adjust to market conditions, factoring in the time element, and integrating oscillator signals into a larger trading plan. These efforts, more than anything, underscore the issues traders should take into account when using oscillators and provide ideas about different ways to apply these indicators more realistically in the markets; they serve as guideposts to further experimentation. Equally clear is that the risks associated with countertrend trading (and its relative value, vis-à-vis trading with the trend) remain intact—it's difficult to overcome such market realities by tweaking an indicator.

One of the most common problems in trading is not seeing the forest for the trees. Technical analysis can confuse traders with a vast array of indicators, impressively titled trade methodologies, complex formulas, and arcane terminology.

Advanced desktop technology can be both a blessing and a curse, as far as analysis is concerned: It puts previously unimaginable power at the fingertips of average traders, but it can also prevent them from getting a hands-on understanding and appreciation of the trading tools with which they attempt to make money. Also, the sheer volume of available market information can result in "analysis paralysis." As one of the most popular groups of trading tools, momentum oscillators are often accepted at face value, their subtleties and finer points—both good and bad—ignored.

No single method or indicator can solve every trading problem, although a seemingly endless supply of people would lead you to believe otherwise (matched by another group ready to believe anything). The glib platitudes that become associated over time with a particular indicator can lead to complacency on the part of the less-experienced user. It's important to investigate the merits of any particular trading approach. Momentum-based indicators can provide unique insights into market behavior. The challenge is to translate these insights into a workable trading plan. The evidence suggests oscillators function better as discretionary or forecasting tools than as the foundation for systematic trading strategies.

# 9

## OTHER
## OSCILLATORS

### A/D OSCILLATOR

Larry Williams and Jim Waters introduced the A/D (Accumulation/Distribution) oscillator in *Commodities* (now *Futures*) magazine in 1972. It uses two intraday momentum calculations, *buying power* and *selling power*, in the following fashion:

Buying power (BP) = high − open

Selling power (SP) = close − low

$$\text{Daily raw figure (DRF)} = \frac{(\text{BP} + \text{SP})}{2 * (\text{high} - \text{low})}$$

The basic oscillator calculation, the daily raw figure (DRF), can be very choppy and may require smoothing to create a usable indicator. Figure 9.1 shows the A/D oscillator with the daily Swiss franc (DRF smoothed with a 20-day average).

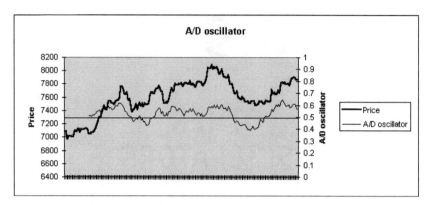

**FIGURE 9.1**    A/D Oscillator with the Daily Swiss Franc

## COMMODITY CHANNEL INDEX

Developed by Donald Lambert and introduced in the October
1980 issue of *Commodities* (now *Futures*) magazine, the commodity channel index (CCI) was actually intended more as a
trend identification or breakout indicator than a countertrend
oscillator. Despite its moniker, it can be applied to any tradable
instrument. The basic CCI trade methodology was essentially
to fade what would be typical oscillator overbought and oversold signals: Buy when the indicator rises above +100 and sell
when the indicator falls below −100. Positions are liquidated
when the indicator retraces these levels and reenters the neutral zone.[1] A quick look reveals the oscillator form of this indicator and the possible interpretation of the +100 and −100
lines as standard overbought/oversold levels. More computa-
tionally complex than most oscillators, the CCI creates an oscillator by comparing price to a mean deviation index of price. The
following calculations are from Lambert's original article.[1]

1. Compute today's "typical" price, using the high, low,
   and close:

$$X_1 = \frac{(H + L + C)}{3}$$

2. Compute a moving average of the $N$ most recent typical prices:

$$\bar{X} = \frac{1}{N}\sum_{i=1}^{N} X_i$$

3. Compute the mean deviation (MD) of the $N$ most recent typical prices:

$$MD = \frac{1}{N}\sum_{i=1}^{N} |X_i - \bar{X}|$$

4. Compute the Commodity Channel Index:

$$CCI = \frac{1.5(X_1 - \bar{X})}{MD}$$

where
$N$ = number of days in data base,
$X_1$ = today's typical price,
$X_2$ = yesterday's typical price,
$X_3$ = day before yesterday's typical price, and
$X_N$ = oldest typical price in data base.

Source: Omega Research

**FIGURE 9.2** Commodity Channel Index

$$\sum_{i=1}^{N}$$ stands for the sum of items following the symbol, starting with 1 and ending with $N$, e.g.,

$$\sum_{i=1}^{N} X_i = X_1 + X_2 + X_3 \ldots + X_N$$

$|\quad|$ = signifies "absolute value"

## DEMARKER INDICATOR

The DeMarker indicator is an unsmoothed momentum tool developed by Tom DeMark that compares the sum of one-day high momentum to the sum of high momentum and low momentum calculated over an $n$-day period.

$$\text{DeMarker indicator} = \frac{\text{SUM(HM)}}{\text{SUM(HM)} + \text{SUM(LM)}},$$

where
HM = one-day high momentum = high today − high yesterday (if today's high is less than or equal to yesterday's high, today's HM value is zero); and
LM = one-day low momentum = low today − low yesterday (if today's low is greater than yesterday's low, today's LM value is zero).

The HM and LM figures are summed over a default period of 13 days and inserted in the formula as shown. The DeMarker indicator ranges from 0 to 100 with standard overbought/oversold levels of 70 and 30, respectively.

## HERRICK PAYOFF INDEX

The Herrick payoff index (developed by James Herrick) uses volume and open interest to monitor the strength and weakness of the "money flow" into and out of a market. Perry Kauf-

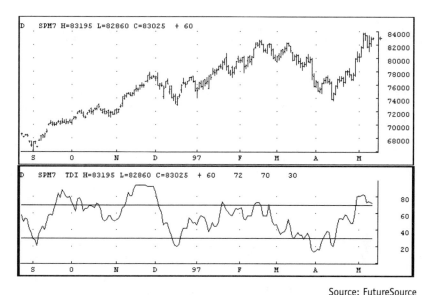

S                 O        N        D        97        F        M        A        M

**FIGURE 9.3**    The DeMarker Indicator

Source: FutureSource

man adapted the following formula from the original published in the early CompuTrac manuals.[2]

$$HPI = HPI[1] + s*(K*HPI[1]),$$

where
HPI is today's Herrick payoff;
HPI[1] is yesterday's value; and
s is a smoothing constant (usually .1).

K is a combination of volume and open interest as follows:

$$K = cf * V * \Delta M * \left( \frac{1 + signM * 2 * abs(\Delta OI)}{min(OI, OI[1])} \right),$$

where
$cf$ is a contract conversion factor ($/pt.) or 100;
V is today's volume;
$\Delta M$ is the one-day change in the mean price $(H - L)/2$;
$signM$ is the sign of $\Delta M$, or, $signM = \Delta M/abs(\Delta M)$. *Note:*
*'signM' is Kaufman's addition to the formula;*

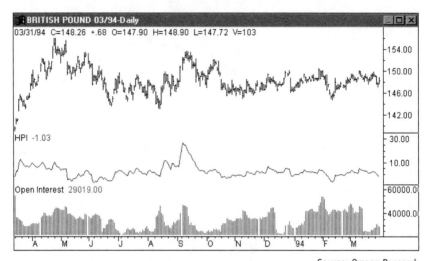

**FIGURE 9.4**    Herrick Payoff Index

ΔOI is the one-day change in open interest;
min(OI,OI[1]) is the smallest of today's or yesterday's open
interest; and
*abs* is absolute value.

K can be divided by 100,000 to scale the value.

## KASECD

Developed by Cynthia Kase, the KaseCD (KCD) is the
PeakOscillator equivalent (see Chapter 6) of the MACD histogram. Whereas the MACD histogram is the difference between the MACD and its moving average (signal line), the
KaseCD is the difference between the PeakOscillator and its
moving average. The PeakOscillator uses a statistical trend
measurement instead of an empirical measurement.

$$KaseCD = PeakOscillator - average(PeakOscillator, n)$$

Figure 9.5 shows the KCD with a standard 12–26–9 MACD.

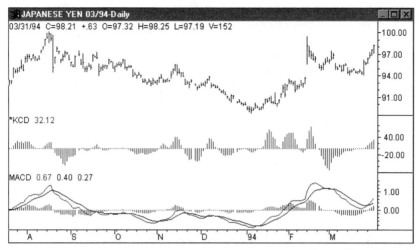

Source: Omega Research

**FIGURE 9.5**  KCD with a Standard 12–26–9 MACD

## PRICE OSCILLATOR

This concept, discussed in Chapter 2, is the basis for the moving average convergence-divergence method: the difference between a shorter moving average and a longer moving average. Variations include the use of exponential or weighted moving averages instead of simple moving averages, and dividing the moving averages instead of subtracting them. This indicator is actually an alternate method of displaying a moving average crossover system.

$$\text{Price oscillator} = MA_1 - MA_2,$$

where
$MA_1$ is a shorter-term moving average (e.g., 10 days); and
$MA_2$ is a longer-term moving average (e.g., 20 days).

The ratio calculation usually divides the difference between the moving averages by the shorter moving average and multiplies the result by 100:

$$\text{Price oscillator} = \left(\frac{MA_1 - MA_2}{MA_1}\right) * 100$$

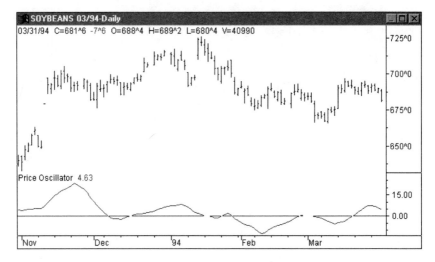

**FIGURE 9.6**   Price Oscillator

## PERCENT R

Larry Williams popularized his Percent R (%R) oscillator in his book *How I Made a Million Dollars Last Year Trading Commodities* (Conceptual Management). The indicator is essentially an inverted calculation of the familiar %K stochastic. Whereas the stochastic compares the difference between the current close and the low over an *n*-day period to the range of that period, %R uses the difference between the *high* of the range and the current close. The default period length is 10 days.

$$\%R = \frac{(H_n - \text{close})}{(H_n - \text{low}_n)},$$

where
$H_n$ = high of *n*-day period;
$\text{low}_n$ = low of *n*-day period; and
close = today's close.

Note that the only difference between this calculation and the stochastic is that the numerator here is the high of the range

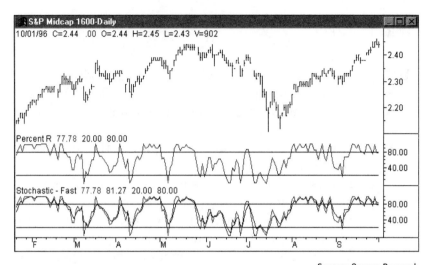

Source: Omega Research

**FIGURE 9.7** Ten-Day %R with a 10-Day Fast Stochastic

minus today's close, whereas the stochastic numerator is today's close minus the low of the range $(C - L_n)$. Figure 9.7 shows the 10-day %R with a 10-day fast stochastic.

## RANGE EXPANSION INDEX

Another unsmoothed indicator developed by Tom DeMark (see "DeMarker Indicator," earlier in this chapter, and Chapter 4 for additional information). The range expansion index (REI) divides two-day high/low momentum by the absolute two-day high/low momentum. The numerator of the calculation is the difference between today's high and the high two days earlier $(H - H_{t-2})$ plus the difference between today's low and the low two days earlier $(L - L_{t-2})$; these daily figures are summed over a default period of five days. The denominator is the sum of the absolute values of the figures in the numerator calculated for the same period ($|H - H_{t-2}| + |L - L_{t-2}|$). The REI ranges from −100 to +100. Default overbought/oversold levels are +45 and −45, respectively.

$$REI = 100 * \left[ \frac{SUM_5\{(H - H_{t-2}) + (L - L_{t-2})\}}{SUM_5\{|(H - H_{t-2}| + |L - L_{t-2}|\}} \right]$$

$SUM_5$ denotes a default five-day calculation period.

Note: To avoid buying or selling into steep declines or advances, these calculations must meet the following criteria:

1. a. H must be greater than or equal to the low five or six days earlier, and
   b. L must be less than or equal to the high five or six days earlier; or
2. a. $H_{t-2}$ must be greater than or equal to the close seven or eight days earlier, and
   b. $L_{t-2}$ must be less than or equal to the close seven or eight days earlier.

If these conditions are not met, the value for that day is zero.

See Chapter 6 for a chart of the REI.

## RELATIVE MOMENTUM INDEX

Developed by Roger Altman and outlined in the February 1993 issue *of Technical Analysis of Stocks and Commodities* magazine, the RMI is basically the RSI calculated on an *n*-day momentum reading (close − close *n* days earlier) rather than one-day momentum (i.e., close − close yesterday).

For example, when calculating an up day for the RSI, yesterday's close is subtracted from today's close (if the result is zero or less, the value for that day is zero). The opposite is calculated for down days.

For the RMI, the up day difference is not calculated between the current bar and the previous bar, but rather between the current bar and the bar *n* days earlier (i.e., *up momentum* and its counterpart, *down momentum*). The trader can adjust this period as desired. For a 5-day momentum calculation, if the close today is higher than the close 5 days ago, the difference between the two becomes the up momentum. If today's close is lower than the close 5 days ago, the up momentum is zero. The reverse calculations are performed to record the down momentum. These figures are summed over a period selected by the user (say, 20 days). The ratio of the up and down momentum is then smoothed using the original RSI technique. The formula is identical to that of the RSI except for one variable:

$$RMI = 100 * \left( \frac{RM}{1 + RM} \right),$$

where
RM = average of the $n$-day up momentum/average of the $n$-day down momentum over $x$ days. [3]

Source: International Pacific Trading Co.

**FIGURE 9.8**    Relative Momentum Index

## ULTIMATE OSCILLATOR

Larry Williams introduced his Ultimate Oscillator in the August 1985 issue of *Technical Analysis of Stocks and Commodities* magazine. The indicator is an example of a concept discussed in Chapter 6: the incorporation of different time cycles in a single oscillator. Williams combines weighted 7-, 14-, and 28-day momentum calculations based on the following price relationships.

1. Calculate today's "buying pressure" (BP).

   BP = Today's close − true low (the lower of today's low or yesterday's close)

2. Calculate today's true range (TR).
   TR is the greatest of:
   a. today's high − today's low;
   b. today's high − yesterday's close;
   c. yesterday's close − today's low.
3. Sum the daily BP figures over the 7-, 14-, and 28-day periods ($BP_7$, $BP_{14}$, $BP_{28}$).

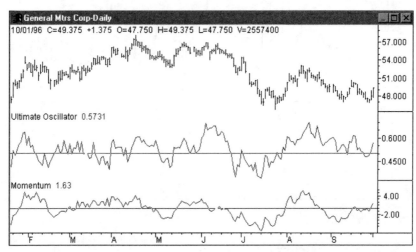

Source: Omega Research

**FIGURE 9.9**    Ultimate Oscillator and Momentum

4. Sum the daily TR figures over the same periods ($TR_7$, $TR_{14}$, $TR_{28}$).
5. Divide the BP sums for each of the periods by the equivalent TR sums ($BP_7/TR_7$, $BP_{14}/TR_{14}$, $BP_{28}/TR_{28}$).
6. Weight the BP/TR ratios as follows:
   a. 4*(BP7/TR7)
   b. 2*(BP14/TR14)
   c. BP28/TR28 (not weighted)

Note: Because the most recent 7 days are used several times in the calculation (being part of the 14- and 28-day periods as well), the indicator is heavily weighted toward this portion of the price data.

# GLOSSARY

Listed are several key words and concepts, as well as a few somewhat obscure topics and references that may benefit from more detailed explanation than appears in the text.

**Acceleration.** The rate at which momentum changes—essentially the momentum of momentum. Acceleration is the first derivative of momentum, which itself is the first derivative of price. It could be expressed as the formula $A = M_t - M_{t-n}$, where $M_t$ is today's momentum and $M_{t-n}$ is the momentum $n$ days ago.

**Adaptive indicators.** Trading tools that change according to market conditions (usually a function of volatility) are referred to as adaptive, or *dynamic*. An example is a moving average that increases or decreases the number of days in its calculation as volatility changes.

**Average directional movement (ADX) index.** Developed by Welles Wilder, the ADX measures trend *strength* rather than *direction*. The formula is too long to include here (it can be found in Wilder's book *New Concepts in Technical Trading*

*Systems*—see bibliography), but the indicator is an expression of the amount of up or down price movement relative to range over a given period. The higher the ADX reading, the stronger the trend presence in the market.

**Divergence.** The failure of an indicator to confirm price action, for example, a new price high accompanied by a lower high in a momentum oscillator, or a steady uptrend accompanied by a consistent momentum decline. Divergence implies price weakness and a possible correction or reversal. The particular phenomenon of nonconfirming price and oscillator extremes is referred to as a *classic divergence*—more specifically, a bearish divergence at market tops and a bullish divergence at market bottoms. But generally, divergence refers to the lack of confirmation between any two comparable instruments, or between an instrument and a benchmark.

**Equilibrium line** (also known as *zero line, median,* or *midpoint*). A horizontal line that marks neutral momentum on an oscillator. Momentum, for example, has an equilibrium line of zero, where the current price is the same as the price *n* days earlier. When the indicator moves above this line, positive momentum is increasing. When the indicator moves below the line, negative momentum is increasing. Equilibrium lines are often used to trigger trend-following trades because directional changes often accompany violations of these lines. On normalized oscillators like the stochastics or the RSI, this line is a midpoint between the upper and lower boundaries, in this case 50—halfway between zero and 100.

**Exponential moving average (EMA).** An exponential moving average is a type of weighted average where a percentage of today's price is applied to yesterday's moving average value: EMA = [close today*smoothing constant] + [previous moving average value*(100 − smoothing constant)].

**Failure swing.** Refers to a pattern when price or a technical indicator makes a new high or low, pulls back, and then makes a second run at the previous extreme and fails to exceed it. It's typically interpreted as a reversal signal; a common trigger is to act when the price (or the indicator) breaks through the pullback level established between the two extremes.

**Fibonacci series.** Named after the 12th-century Italian mathematician who discovered it, the Fibonacci series is the progression of numbers in which each consecutive member is the sum of the preceding two numbers, such as 1, 1, 2, 3, 5, 8, 13, 21, 34 ($1 + 2 = 3, 2 + 3 = 5, 3 + 5 = 8, 5 + 8 = 13, 8 + 13 = 21, 13 + 21 = 34$, etc.). The progression of numbers in this series appears throughout natural phenomena as diverse as the spiral growth of snail shells and the development of tree leaves. As the series progresses, the ratio of a number in the series divided by the preceding number approaches 1.618—the "golden mean" found in the dimensions of the Parthenon and the Great Pyramid (the inverse, .618, obtained by dividing a Fibonacci number by its succeeding number, has similar significance). Many traders tie market events to cycles of Fibonacci numbers and ratios, using them in time projections and price forecasts and as period lengths for indicators.

**Key reversal day.** A pattern that occurs when price makes a new high (preferably an extreme high or spike top) but the market closes at or near the bottom of the daily range. The implication is that the market has blown off steam at the top, and the low close indicates sellers are settling in on the market. The pattern is reversed at market bottoms (new market low, high close).

**Lead.** In the context of momentum, the tendency of momentum-based indicators to foreshadow price developments, for example, reversing before price itself reverses. Commonly referred to as the *leading characteristic*. Smoothing techniques like moving averages produce the opposite effect, *lag*.

**Momentum.** As a generic term, momentum refers to the rate at which prices change over time—the speed of the market—

rather than the absolute difference between price levels. Momentum also is a specific calculation: the price today minus the price $n$ days earlier ($P_t - P_{t-n}$). See also **acceleration.**

**Normalized.** Indicators that are calculated to fall within a fixed range are referred to as normalized. Popular examples include the stochastic indicator and the RSI, which both range between 0 and 100. By comparison, indicators like momentum and the MACD have no upper or lower boundaries.

**Overbought/Oversold**: Refer to a market that has risen or fallen too far too fast (an *overextended* or *exhausted* price move) and is thus ripe for a correction. Specific overbought and oversold oscillator values (like 70 and 30 for the 14-day RSI) are designed to coincide with (and more importantly, give advance warning of) such exhaustion points in price and are referred to as overbought/oversold levels, or thresholds (also referred to as **extreme thresholds;** the areas above and below established oscillator overbought/oversold levels are sometimes referred to as **extreme zones**).

**Period length.** The number of time units used to calculate an indicator. Also referred to as the *lookback* or *lookback period.* A 10-day RSI has a period length of 10; a 24-month moving average has a period length of 24. The longer the period length, the longer the time cycle or trend the indicator will reflect.

**Serial dependency.** A statistical term analogous to the concept of trend. Refers to a time series that shows a degree of connection, or positive feedback, that statistically exceeds what a random series would be expected to produce. A nonrandom, or trending, price series exhibits serial dependency.

**Signal line.** A moving average of an indicator that functions as a trade trigger. A trade is indicated when the oscillator passes above or below its signal line (in the same manner in which trades are triggered when price violates its moving average). The MACD, Blau's ergodic oscillator, and the stochastic oscillator are examples of indicators that incorporate such signal lines.

**Stop-and-reverse.** Stop-and-reverse refers to a trading system that is always "in the market." For example, when the system indicates an exit from a long trade, two sales are immediately executed: one that offsets (stops out) the long position and another that simultaneously establishes a new short position. The process is repeated at the next long signal—the system is never flat.

**Trailing stop.** A stop that follows a position as it advances rather than remaining at a fixed level. A five-point trailing stop on a long position, for example, is always five points below the current position. Commonly used as a method to protect open-trade profits.

**Trading range.** A nontrending market that fluctuates in a relatively defined range. Oscillators perform better in trading range markets because they are not subject to the repeated false signals that can occur in a trending market. A related term is *congested market,* in which prices move in a very tight, almost static horizontal trading range.

**True range.** Another Welles Wilder concept, true range is a common volatility measurement calculated as the greatest of the absolute distances between:

1. today's high and today's low;
2. yesterday's close and today's high;
3. yesterday's close and today's low.

The *average true range* (ATR) is simply the true range averaged over a particular time period.

**Whipsaw.** Refers to the phenomenon of price moving quickly and repeatedly above and below a trade trigger like a moving average, resulting in a series of alternating false buy-and-sell signals. The same term refers to the behavior of an indicator moving back and forth over a trade trigger, such as an oscillator repeatedly crossing its equilibrium line or its overbought or oversold thresholds.

# NOTES

## CHAPTER 2

1. Robert F. Colby and Thomas A. Meyers, *The Encyclopedia of Technical Market Indicators* (Homewood, IL: Dow Jones-Irwin, 1988), p. 361.

## CHAPTER 5

1. Charles LeBeau and David W. Lucas, *Technical Traders Guide to Computer Analysis of the Futures Market* (Homewood, IL: Dow Jones-Irwin,1992), pp. 173–185.
2. Colby and Meyers, pp. 414–476.

## CHAPTER 6

1. Tushar Chande and Stanley Kroll, *The New Technical Trader* (New York: John Wiley & Sons, 1994), pp. 95–108.
2. Tom DeMark, *The New Science of Technical Analysis* (New York: John Wiley & Sons, 1994), p. 93
3. Chande and Kroll, pp. 8–9.
4. Martin J. Pring, *Martin Pring on Market Momentum* (Gloucester, Va.: Martin Pring/International Institute for Economic Research, 1993), pp. 151–153.

5. Ibid., pp. 153–157.

6. Ibid., pp. 161–164.

7. Chande and Kroll, p. 134.

8. Ibid., p. 135.

9. Ibid., p. 135.

10. E. Marshall Wall, "Rolling With the Punches," *Futures,* July 1996, pp. 38–40.

11. John Ehlers, "Leading Indicators with Momentum," *Technical Analysis of Stocks & Commodities,* September 1989, pp. 78–80.

12. William Blau, *Momentum, Direction, and Divergence* (New York: John Wiley & Sons, 1995), pp. 13–14.

13. Ibid., p. 66.

14. Ibid., p. 16.

15. Ibid., p. 33.

16. Ibid., p. 17.

17. Ibid., pp. 5–17.

18. Ibid., p. 53.

19. Ibid., pp. 22–23.

20. E. Michael Poulos, "Of Trends and Random Walks," *Technical Analysis of Stocks & Commodities*, February 1991, pp. 26–31.

21. Ibid., p. 30.

22. Ibid.

23. E. Michael Poulos, "Futures According to Trend Tendency," *Technical Analysis of Stocks & Commodities*, January 1992, pp. 61–66.

24. Cynthia Kase, *Trading with the Odds: Using the Power of Probability to Profit in the Futures Market* (Chicago: Business One–Irwin Professional Publishing, 1996), pp. 77–78.

25. Ibid., p. 78.

26. Tom DeMark, *The New Science of Technical Analysis* (New York: John Wiley & Sons, 1994), p. 89.

27. Ibid.

## CHAPTER 7

1. Blau, p. 103.

2. LeBeau and Lucas, p. 126.

3. Pring, pp. 16–17.

4. Ibid.

5. LeBeau and Lucas, pp. 70–71.

6. William Brower, "Can Divergence Help Predict Market Moves?" *TS Express*, November/December 1995, pp. 5–8.

7. LeBeau and Lucas, p. 72.

## CHAPTER 9

1. Donald R. Lambert, "Commodity Channel Index: Tool for Trading Cyclic Trends," *Commodities* (now *Futures*), October 1980, pp. 40–41.

2. *Futures*, May 1995, p.10.

3. Roger Altman, "The Relative Momentum Index: Modifying RSI," *Technical Analysis of Stocks & Commodities*, February 1993, p. 30.

# BIBLIOGRAPHY

## BOOKS

Achelis, Steven B. *Technical Analysis from A to Z*. Chicago: Probus, 1995.

Babcock, Bruce. *Business One–Irwin Guide to Trading Systems*. Chicago: Business One–Irwin, 1989.

Bernstein, Jake. *Timing Signals in the Futures Market: The Trader's Definitive Guide to Buy/Sell Indicators*. Chicago: Probus, 1992.

Blau, William. *Momentum, Direction and Divergence*. New York: John Wiley & Sons, 1995.

Chande, Tushar, and Stanley Kroll. *The New Technical Trader*. New York: John Wiley & Sons, 1994.

Colby, Robert F., and Thomas A. Meyers. *The Encyclopedia of Technical Market Indicators*. Homewood, IL: Dow Jones-Irwin, 1988.

DeMark, Tom. *The New Science of Technical Analysis*. New York: John Wiley & Sons, 1994

———. *New Market Timing Techniques*. New York: John Wiley & Sons, 1997.

Kase, Cynthia. *Trading with the Odds: Using the Power of Probability to Profit in the Futures Market*. Chicago: Business One–Irwin Professional, 1996.

Kaufman, Perry. *The New Commodity Trading Systems and Methods*. New York: John Wiley & Sons, 1987.

LeBeau, Charles, and David W. Lucas. *Technical Traders Guide to Computer Analysis of the Futures Market*. Homewood, IL: Dow Jones-Irwin, 1992.

Murphy, John. *Technical Analysis in the Futures Markets*. New York: New
    York Institute of Finance/Prentice Hall, 1986.
Pring, Martin J. *Martin Pring on Market Momentum*. Gloucester, Va.: Mar-
    tin Pring/International Institute for Economic Research, 1993..
Schwager, Jack. *Schwager on Futures: Technical Analysis*. New York: John
    Wiley & Sons, 1996.
Wilder, J. Welles Jr. *New Concepts in Technical Trading Systems*. Greens-
    boro, N.C.: J. Welles Wilder Jr./Trend Research, 1978.

## ARTICLES

Aan, Peter W. "How RSI Behaves." *Futures*, January 1985, p. 76.
Altman, Roger. "The Relative Momentum Index: Modifying RSI." *Technical
    Analysis of Stocks & Commodities*, February 1993, pp. 30–35.
Blau, William. "Trading With the True Strength Index." *Technical Analysis
    of Stocks & Commodities*, May 1992, pp. 62–69.
Brower, William. "Can Divergence Help Predict Market Moves?" *TS Ex-
    press*, November/December 1995, pp. 1–8.
Ehlers, John. "Leading Indicators with Momentum." *Technical Analysis of
    Stocks & Commodities*, September 1989, pp. 78–80.
Kase, Cynthia. "New High-Probability Indicators Combining Statistics
    with Technical Analysis." *Metals in the News*, Spring 1996, pp. 1–6.
Poulos, E. Michael. "Of Trends and Random Walks." *Technical Analysis of
    Stocks & Commodities*, February 1991, pp. 26–31.
———. "Futures According to Trend Tendency." *Technical Analysis of
    Stocks & Commodities*, January 1992, pp. 61–66.
———"Taking A New Look At Baffling Price Moves." *Futures*, April 1992,
    pp. 30–32.
Pring, Martin. "Identifying Trends with the KST Indicator." *Technical
    Analysis of Stocks & Commodities,* October 1992, pp. 54–59.
Storz, Matt. "Quantifying Divergence with the Divergence Index." *Techni-
    cal Analysis of Stocks and Commodities*, January 1996, pp. 40–44.
Wall, E. Marshall. "Rolling With the Punches." *Futures*, July 1996, pp.
    38–40.

## ADDITIONAL READING

Babcock, Bruce. *Profitable Commodity Trading from A to Z. CTCR: The
    First Ten Years.* Sacramento: Advanced Trading Seminars, 1994.
———. *The Four Cardinal Principles of Trading*. Chicago: Business
    One–Irwin Professional, 1996.
Chande, Tushar. *Beyond Technical Analysis*. New York: John Wiley & Sons,
    1997.

Kaufman, Perry. *Smarter Trading.* New York: McGraw-Hill, 1995.

Mackay, Charles. *Extraordinary Popular Delusions and the Madness of Crowds.* New York: Marketplace Books/John Wiley & Sons, 1996.

Murphy, John. *Intermarket Technical Analysis.* New York: John Wiley & Sons, 1991.

Pardo, Robert. *Design, Testing and Optimization of Trading Systems.* New York: John Wiley & Sons, 1992.

Rotella, Robert. *The Elements of Successful Trading.* New York: New York Institute of Finance, 1992.

Schwager, Jack. *Schwager on Futures: Fundamental Analysis.* New York: John Wiley & Sons, 1995.

———. *Market Wizards.* New York: New York Institute of Finance, 1989.

———. *The New Market Wizards.* New York: HarperBusiness, 1992.

Smith, Gary. *Live the Dream by Profitably Day Trading Stock Index Futures.* Sacramento, CA: Advanced Trading Seminars, Inc., 1995.

# INDEX